AL...

in your pocket

Len Port

VISTA IBÉRICA

Vista Ibérica Publicações, Portugal
Tel. 00351 282 340660 · Fax. 00351 282 343088
Email: lenport@mail.telepac.pt

THIRD EDITION, WHOLLY REVISED 2004.
First published 1995
Second edition 1999

Copyright   Text © Len Port 1995-2003
                     Photographs © Len Port and Joan Gay

Publisher   Published by Vista Ibérica Publicações,
                     Urb. Lagoa Sol, 1B, 8400 Lagoa, Portugal.
                     Tel. (00351) 282 340660.
                     Fax (00351) 282 343088
                     Email: lenport@mail.telepac.pt

Page setting   Paula Duarte

Printer   Phalempin - Indústria Gráfica, S.A.

ISBN: 972-8044-09-7   *Depósito legal:* 212794/04

Every effort has been made to ensure the information in this
book is as accurate and up-to-date as possible at the time of
going to press. Details, however, are liable to change. The author
and publisher can accept no responsibility for legal claims or
problems of any kind arising from any inaccuracies or omissions.

NEXT EDITION: We would be pleased to receive from readers any
suggestions for updates, changes or inclusions in the next
edition.

OTHER BOOKS BY THE SAME AUTHOR AND PUBLISHERS:
                     Get to know the Algarve
                     Algarve on Wheels
                     Bica the Portuguese Water Dog
                     Best Photo Guide to the Algarve
                     Algarve Images

CONTENTS

JUST FOR STARTERS

Let's clear up a common misconception: on arrival, you are IN the Algarve not ON it. This is not an island. Nor is it one of the Spanish *costas*. The Algarve is not in Spain. It's in Portugal.

All this is obvious, you may say. Maybe to you, but not to half the people who come here. Many holidaymakers don't seem to know where they are. Places with sun, sea and sand, and maybe a bit of sex thrown in, all look the same to some people. They aren't. The Algarve is not only special, it's unique.

As Portugal's southernmost province, the Algarve is geographically distinct in character from the rest of Europe and, indeed, from the rest of Portugal.

The climate is classified as 'Mediterranean' in type, like that in Spain and the rest of southern Europe and North Africa. That means long summers, mild winters and a modest rainfall, nearly all of which falls during the cooler months. Because of the influences of the ocean to the south and west and hills along its northern boundary, the Algarve is

---

PORTUGAL IN POETRY

"Oh, Christ! It is a goodly sight to see
What Heaven hath done for this delicious land!
What fruits of fragrance blush on every tree!
What goodly prospects o'er the hills expand."

Lord Byron on his visit to Portugal in 1809

Praia D'Ana, Lagos

blessed with a micro-climate which is more mellow and equable than the rest of Portugal and Spain. For example, ocean breezes usually prevent it from becoming unpleasantly hot, even at the height of summer. The northern hills shield against biting winds in winter.

There is an abundance of sunshine all year round. In fact, the Algarve probably has more sunshine each year that anywhere else in Europe. You have to go to the desert countries of Africa or halfway round the world to California to get as much.

Around Christmas it can pour with rain, but you often get exhilarating, crystal-clear days when the distant mountains are etched in purple and the sky is not just blue, it's brilliant, vivid blue and you can look for a wisp of cloud and not find one. If you live here, it's then more than at any other time of the year that you realise this really is a very special place to be.

During the winter, while the rugged-up masses in northern Europe are still coping with snowdrifts, black ice and freezing fog, visitors to the Algarve can be gently soaking up suntans while playing rounds of golf in short sleeves. There are more than two dozen immaculate golf courses strung out along the south coast - 'golf's golden coast' - and they add up to the most concentrated and diverse set of golfing challenges on the Continent.

Spring comes to the Algarve even before the old year is out. For example, one of its most flamboyant birds, the hoopoe, is usually sitting on a clutch of

Winter almond blossom

eggs at the end of December when the first almond blossom bursts forth and starts to run riot all over the countryside.

Early and late summer are the preferred periods for the growing number of visitors attracted by the Algarve's cultural traditions, its easy-going lifestyle, its tumultuous history, its extraordinary rich and varied wildlife, plus all sorts of sports and leisure activities that may be best enjoyed in the absence of crowds. These are the seasons for exploring the inland villages, farmlands, foothills and forested *serras* which so perfectly complement the dune and cliff-sculptured coastline.

The coast is the place to be in high summer when the sunshiny days seem to go on and on forever. It is a strikingly beautiful coast, partly because it is shaped and washed not by the enclosed Mediterranean Sea, but by the open Atlantic.

The Algarve's beaches come in all shapes and sizes, from intimate coves to vast, open strands. Whether you like strolling along, planting a line of footsteps on soft virgin sand, or sizzling sardine-like in serried ranks of bronzing bodies, you won't find beaches more beautiful or better suited to bathing anywhere in the northern hemisphere this side of the Caribbean.

Seaside towns and villages, like the beaches next to them, come in many forms, ranging from dozy fishing hamlets, through teeming resorts to custom-designed complexes tailored for the rich and famous. Wherever you are staying or visiting, there is nothing wrong with lolling about on a beach or next to a pool by day and relaxing in a restaurant or bar at night, so long as you don't feel you are missing out on scuba-diving or art classes, windsurfing or line dancing, jet-skiing or live classical music, paragliding or lawn bowls, horse riding or bridge. We could go on….

Some people come to the Algarve and don't make any bigger decision than whether to open a bottle of red wine or white. And that's all right too: although there are lots of activities to tempt you, there is no better place to chill out and flip-flop around doing nothing. The Algarve is hospitable and friendly. Whatever you do or don't do, you won't feel ill at ease - and you will almost certainly want to come back at the end of it all.

The village of Ferragudo, opposite Portimão

JUST FOR STARTERS

WHEN TO VISIT?

If you have a choice of seasons or months, consider the following pros and cons:

July and August - warm, sometimes very, no rain. Best sea and sunbathing. Masses of activity.

But: *Top accommodation and car hire prices. Advance booking almost essential. Heaviest traffic and crowds.*

March to June - Warm, very little rain. Countryside and coast at its most beautiful best. Top time for naturalists, bikers, walkers.

But: *Sea chilly. Getting busy and pricey, especially over Easter.*

September and October - Still warm, little rain. Accommodation prices have dropped, crowds thinned out.

But: *Countryside dried out, hotel and restaurant staff getting tired out.*

November to February - Mild and often sunny. Peace and quiet. Accommodation prices rock bottom. Best time for golfers, long-stay visitors and those on very tight budgets.

But: *This is when the rain falls and it does so erratically, occasionally for prolonged periods. Maybe too much peace and quiet. Many bars and restaurants closed.*

WHERE TO STAY?

LOCATIONS

Every town, village and rural area in the Algarve has its own individual atmosphere and special attractions. This diversity is one of the great features of southern Portugal.

By far the most popular sec-

AIR TEMPERATURES

	Jan	Feb	Mar	Apr	May	Jun	Jul	Aug	Sep	Oct	Nov	Dec
Max. °C	15	17	19	21	24	27	31	31	29	22	18	16
Min. °C	8	10	11	12	14	18	17	17	16	15	13	11

• *these are mean daytime maximum and night-time minimum air temperatures measured in the shade at the Centre for Observational Astronomy, near Portimão.*

SEA TEMPERATURES

	Jan	Feb	Mar	Apr	May	Jun	Jul	Aug	Sep	Oct	Nov	Dec
°C	15	15	15	16	17	18	19	20	20	19	17	16

The rugged west coast

tion of the south coast is between Faro and Lagos (Chapter 4), where sweeping bays are interspersed by lovely little coves and fantastic rock formations. East of Faro (Chapter 6), the coastline is much less developed and scenically more placid. West of Lagos (Chapter 5) it is little developed, but scenically dramatic.

EAST TO WEST:

Beachside towns: Tavira, Albufeira, Lagos.

Other main towns: Vila Real de St° António, Olhão, Faro, Loulé, Portimão.

Smaller towns: São Brás de Alportel, São Bartolomeu de Messines, Lagoa, Silves, Monchique.

Big beachside villages: Monte Gordo, Quarteira, Armação de Pera, Carvoeiro, Praia da Rocha,

Quiet beachside villages: Olhos d'Água, Ferragudo, Alvor, Luz, Burgau, Salema, Sagres, Odeceixe.

Big developments: Quinta do Lago, Vale do Lobo, Vilamoura.

ACCOMMODATION

There is the widest possible range of accommodation. Apart from the many hotels, inns and guesthouses, there is plenty of self-catering accommodation in holiday villas, apartments and aparthotels. There are also many campsites.

Hotels, inns and guesthouses are all officially star-rated. Tourist complexes are also classified. Prices are competitive and reflect the standard of accommodation.

WHAT TO TAKE?

TRAVEL DOCUMENTS

EU citizens need only passports. The same goes for holidaying Australians, New Zealanders, Canadians and Americans. Other nationalities should check with a travel company or Portuguese embassy to see if they need a visa.

DRIVING LICENCE

Any national or international licence will do, but it must be valid and carried in the vehicle with you along with ownership/rental and insurance papers.

MEDICAL INSURANCE

There are reciprocal arrangements between Portugal and other EU countries on free state medical treatment in emergencies. Even so, travel insurance is always advisable.

MONEY

Foreign cash and travellers' cheques can easily be exchanged for the euro currency used in Portugal. Credit cards are widely accepted, but not all restaurants, for example, accept them.

CLOTHING

Casual clothing is the custom everywhere in the Algarve. In summer, cotton, not synthetic material, is best. A hat is important. In winter you will need some warm clothing, especially in the evening.

SPORTS EQUIPMENT

You may want to bring your own specialised equipment, but such things as golf clubs, tennis rackets, scuba-diving gear, windsurfers and mountain bikes can all be hired locally.

MEDICATION

By far the commonest health risk is sunburn. All the usual blocking or soothing creams are readily available.

Bring any special medication you have to take regularly, but in emergencies you will find that Portuguese pharmacies are sophisticated and well stocked for all normal needs.

No inoculations are required to visit Portugal.

PAST AND PRESENT

INVADERS

Several centuries before Christ, the **Phoenicians** from city-states on the coast of what is now Syria and Lebanon set up trading posts in the Algarve as they had done all along the Mediterranean. They were particularly interested in mining inland deposits of Iberian tin, copper and silver. The **Carthaginians** took over from the Phoenicians and, under the great generals Hamilcar and Hannibal, established an empire of which the Algarve formed the extreme west.

After the **Romans** defeated the Carthaginians in the Second Punic War (218-202BC) they absorbed southern Portugal into their empire. The Romans firmly implanted their language, laws and culture and remained the dominant power throughout Portugal

WHAT'S IN A NAME?

*The name 'Algarve' is one of the legacies of Moorish rule in southern Iberia. Derived from the Arabic **al-Garb**, it means 'the west'. The name was apt in medieval times because of the region's position relative to the rest of the vast Islamic empire. Muslim Portugal was ruled from al-Andalus, now the neighbouring Spanish province of Andalusia, but the Algarve had its own prosperous regional capital at Chelb, now Silves. Plenty of other Algarve place names are derived from Arabic origins: Albufeira, Almancil, Aljezur and Alcoutim, to name but a few.*

Temple of Diana, Évora

for 500 years. The main Roman town in the Algarve was Ossanóba, probably on the site of present-day Faro.

The Romans also introduced a new religion: Christianity. It replaced paganism in the Algarve in the second or third century AD. In the fifth century, Germanic tribes swept through the Roman empire. The Suevi and the Vandals fought one another to gain power in northern and central Portugal but a larger tribe, the **Visigoths**, eventually superseded them and penetrated to the far south. The influence of the Visigoths in the Algarve was neither great nor lasting and, when serious divisions broke out between them, they were a push-over for a new wave of invaders who arrived in the eighth century from North Africa.

The new occupiers were a mixture of Arabs and Berbers known as the **Moors**. Their religion was Islam and they brought with them an entirely different culture. Within a decade of their arrival in the year 712, the Moors had conquered almost all of Portugal, as well as Spain. They settled throughout most of the Iberian peninsula, but preferred the south where they dominated the economic and cultural life for well over five centuries.

There were times of terrible conflict between the occupying Muslim Moors and the indigenous Christian Portuguese. For long periods, though, the Moors were tolerant of their non-Muslim subjects, Jews as well as Christians, allowing freedom of worship, observance of local civil laws and certain land rights. The fire of Christianity and nationalism, however, was inextinguishable.

There was on-going distrust if not outright conflict between Portugal and her Spanish neighbours. Portugal became a nation state by securing its **independence** from the Spanish kingdom of León in 1128. Meanwhile, the Christian 're-conquest', which began in the north of the country, proceeded slowly and relentlessly southward. Moorish resistance persisted longest in the Algarve. It was finally overcome in 1253. The king who completed the job and unified the whole country was Afonso III. He was crowned "King of Portugal and the Algarve".

The southernmost province has always been considered different to the rest of the country, but since 1253 it has always been an integral part of the Portuguese nation.

NATIONHOOD

Friction between Portugal and the Spanish kingdom of Castile continued after the expulsion of the Moors in the south. England sided squarely with Portugal. In the vital Battle of Aljubarrota in central Portugal, 500 English archers fought alongside Portuguese forces and helped bring about a momentous victory. The Portuguese-English alliance was sealed by the **Treaty of Windsor** and further cemented by the marriage between Portugal's King João I and Philippa of Lancaster, daughter of John of Gaunt. The Treaty of Windsor, the longest alliance between any two countries in history, is still in existence today.

João I and Phillipa founded Portugal's most illustrious dynasty, the House of Aviz. Their third surviving son,

TREATY OF WINDSOR

The 1386 treaty between Portugal and England pledged: "an inviolable, eternal, strong perpetual and true league of friendship, alliance and union, not only between each other, their heirs and successors, but also between and in favour of their kingdoms, lands, dominions and subjects, vassals, allies and friends, wherever they may be, so that all of them shall be under the obligation to aid the other against all people now born or to be born who may seek to violate the peace of others or in anyway offend their states."

during the **Age of Discovery**. The greatest achievements came after Henry's death: rounding the Cape of Good Hope in 1488, pushing through the sea route to India a decade later, and claiming Brazil for the Portuguese crown in 1500. This was an epoch of achievement unsurpassed in Portuguese history.

Portugal was able to cash in on its supremacy at sea, monopoly of the oriental spice trade, and control of Europe's first great overseas empire which stretched from Brazil to China, from the Atlantic islands of Azores and Madeira to India and the Malay peninsula. But its days of glory and great wealth did not last for long. By about 1550, the economy was already in steep

Henry, was to become known as '**Henry the Navigator**', instigator and master-mind of voyages into the unknown

HENRY THE NAVIGATOR

King Jõao I appointed his third son, Prince Henry, then 25-years-old, as Governor of the Algarve in 1419. From then until his death at the age of 66, Henry spent much of his time at Lagos and Sagres masterminding voyages that had three main objectives: to push back the frontiers of geographical knowledge, expand trade and spread the Christian religion. Henry was not himself a great mariner. In fact, he rarely went to sea and only on short or coastal voyages. Popular mythology has always masked a complex and enigmatic personality. For example, Henry was both extraordinaryily devout and vain. His monumental contribution to the Age of Discovery, however, was the exceptional vision, determination and organisational skills he brought to bear.

EPIC STORY OF HEROES

"This is the story of heroes who, leaving their native Portugal behind them, opened a way to Ceylon, and further, across seas no man had ever sailed before. They were men of no ordinary stature, equally at home in war and in dangers of every kind: they founded a new kingdom among distant peoples, and made it great. It is the story too of a line of kings who kept ever advancing the boundaries of faith and empire, spreading havoc among the infidels of Africa and Asia and achieving immortality through their illustrious exploits. If my inspiration but prove equal to the task, all men shall know of them."

The opening lines of *The Lusiads*, Portugal's most celebrated piece of literature, by **Luis Vaz de Camões**, known in English as Camoens. *The Lusiads*, an epic narrative poem in ten cantos, describes the heroic figure of Vasco da Gama and his pioneering voyage to India. It was first published in 1572.

decline. The high cost of maintaining grants and privileges at home, and administrating colonies and running trading posts abroad, were more than offset by falling prices for oriental wares and the loss of lucrative monopolies to the

CARAVELS

The caravel was a revolutionary type of sailing vessel developed in the 15th century. It was light, fast and highly manoeuvrable, but most significantly of all, and unlike any previous craft, it was capable of sailing into the wind. This meant it was ideal for the long voyages between Portugal and the west coast of Africa. Typically with two or three masts, caravels were 'lateen rigged' meaning they had triangular-shaped sails on sloping yardarms. The Niña and Pinta, two of Colombus' ships on the first voyage to the New World in 1492, were caravels.

French, the English and the Dutch.

Years of exploration, expansiveness and exuberance were replaced by the **Inquisition**. The throne was occupied by a 'boy king', **Sebastião**, who set off from the shores of the Algarve in 1578 with 500 ships and a substantial army on a latter-day crusade to Morocco. His army was routed. The king and thousands of his troops were killed.

Shortly after Sebastião's death, his elderly and celibate uncle, a cardinal, also died. Thus, the House of Aviz ended in ignominy. The Portuguese then suffered the humiliation of falling under **Spanish rule.** It was 60 years before Portugal regained its independence.

The Braganza dynasty assumed power as Portugal recovered its kingdom and some of its empire, most notably Brazil. The first half of the 18th century was characterized by great pomp and splendour as riches, mostly in the form of gold and diamonds, poured in from the colonies. Behind this veil of prosperity, however, lay a nation in decline. Then came two devastating events: The **Great Lisbon Earthquake** (1755) and three successive invasions by Napoleon. Portugal and Britain were close allies in the so-called **Penin-**

THE GREAT EARTHQUAKE

The earthquake that struck southern Portugal on November 1 1755, All Saints' Day, is usually called the 'Great Lisbon Earthquake'. Its epicentre, in fact, was closer to the Algarve than Lisbon, but both places were devastated. It was the worst earthquake ever recorded in Europe. Nearly every church and most other buildings of any size or importance collapsed or were severely damaged by fire or tidal waves. The death toll may have been as many as 60,000.

The first and strongest of three massive shocks struck at 9.40am as Roman Catholic masses were being held throughout the country. The fact that so many of those who died were at prayer led to intense soul-searching in Portugal and debate throughout Europe. Had the earthquake been a natural disaster, or an expression of God's wrath?

sular **War** against the French. It ended when Sir Arthur Wellesley, later Duke of Wellington, expelled the French from Portugal in 1811 and from Spain three years later.

The French Revolution had given Portuguese dissidents ideas of their own. A democratic movement took root and led to a successful revolution in Oporto in 1820. It spread to other parts of the country, shattering the nation's ancient political structure. Brazil declared its independence. Serious civil unrest simmered and eventually erupted into the **War of the Two Brothers,** with Liberals and their English-style democratic constitution on one side and Conservatives (or Absolutists) who supported royal authority and the establishment on the other.

THE REPUBLIC

In 1910, a republican movement overthrew Manuel II, whose father and eldest brother had been assassinated two years earlier. The leaders of the movement were academics, professional men and military officers who hoped to stabilise the nation's chaotic economy by suppressing both the monarchy and the Roman Catholic

Salazar

Church. Instead, the economic chaos continued because of internal turmoil. It worsened with the outbreak of **World War I.**

At the outset of the War, Portugal remained neutral. It entered the fray by confiscating German shipping in Portuguese ports in 1916. The years following the war were filled with political demonstrations, strikes, violence against individual political leaders, collapsed governments and attempted coups. From this maelstrom emerged one of Portugal's most famous and controversial leaders of all time: **Dr António de Oliviera Salazar.**

Salazar was professor of economics at the University

of Coimbra, Portugal's oldest university, when he was asked to take on the key job of finance minister. As such, he was extraordinarily successful in directing Portugal along the road to financial recovery. In 1932, he became prime minister and soon set up a **'New State'** constitution which gave him dictatorial powers. The idea of the New State was to end the decades of destructive political turmoil and create harmony under a one-party, authoritian regime.

When **World War II** broke out Portugal, by agreement with its old ally Britain, officially remained neutral. However, from 1943 to the end of the war, British and United States forces were allowed to use an air base in the mid-Atlantic Azores group of islands to protect Allied merchant shipping from German U-boat attacks.

While the Second World War had left Portugal largely unscathed, it was convulsed in the early 1960s by **guerilla wars** in its African colonies. They raged on three fronts: Angola, Mozambique and Portuguese Guinea. Portugal pumped man-power and money into combating popular movements fighting for national independence, all to no avail. Drained after 13 years

of fighting, peace abroad was brought about by insurrection at home.

REVOLUTION

At thirty minutes past midnight on **25th April 1974**, Radio Renascença, a Lisbon station, played a popular piece of music called *Grandola, Vila Morena*. To those in the know, it was the pre-arranged signal to stage a military coup against the right-wing government of Salazar's successor, Marcello Caetano.

Before light, all the key buildings in the capital and the provinces were occupied by rebel troops. The international airports of Lisbon, Oporto and Faro were closed. There was virtually no resistance and very little bloodshed. The 'Revolution' had been a well-planned and classically executed coup d'etat led by disaffected young officers, mostly captains and majors. It brought the people of Portugal out into the streets in celebration for they, too, desperately wanted change after 40 years of dictatorship.

Free speech and party politics returned with a vengeance. Business confidence and capital took flight as major industries were nationalised. Many family firms and large country estates were taken over by the workers. Almost a million citizens arrived from the war-torn former Portuguese territories in Africa. The mid-1970s were tumultuous times.

In the immediate **post-revolution** years, the centre-left Socialist Party of Mário Soares vied with the Communists for control, but by 1979 the centre-right Social Democrats were in the ascendancy. One elected coalition government after another collapsed. In July 1987, the Social Democrats (PSD) achieved the first overall parliamentary majority since the revolution. Subsequent elections have been closely fought by the PSD and Socialists. They remain the two dominant political parties.

Portugal, a founder member of NATO, joined the **European Community** in 1986 and enthusiastically introduced the **euro** single currency at the beginning of 2002.

PORTUGAL TODAY

Portugal is a little larger in land area than Scotland or the Republic of Ireland. It has a **population** of a little under 10.5 million. About 30% of the population lives in urban areas, the biggest cities being Lisbon and Oporto. It is a relatively young population.

Politically, Portugal is a **parliamentary democracy** with a President as head-of-state. Parliamentarians are elected every five years in a system of proportional representation. The President holds significant overall powers, but he is not concerned with day-to-day administration. That is left to the Prime Minister and his government.

In recent years, much of the government's most urgent attention has been focused on the state of the country's **economy**. Before enlargement of the EU in 2003, Portugal was Europe's poorest country with wages lagging well behind other members. By emphasizing the need for better education, more professional training, higher productivity and greater competitiveness, Portugal aspires to living standards in line with the best in the EU, but that is probably still some way off.

PAST AND PRESENT

Fisherman

THE ALGARVE TODAY

Up to a few decades ago, before tourists discovered the Algarve, livelihoods in the southern province were based on **fishing** and **farming**.

A huge array of fish and shellfish are brought in every morning and sold fresh in town and village markets. The problem for local fishermen nowadays, however, is that while tourism has hugely increased the demand, catches have been greatly reduced because of over-fishing, as they have everywhere else.

The once hugely important tuna fishing industry has collapsed altogether. An even more startling measure of the decline in the fishing industry is that nearly all of the frantically busy sardine canning factories that once exported to the world are now closed and derelict. Still, there never seems to be a shortage of fresh sardines, plump and ready for the charcoal grill.

Farming is on the wane. Even so, the big-five traditional crops (grapes, olives, almonds, figs and carobs) are still widely grown and harvested using ancestral methods. There are many oranges and lemon orchards, especially in the foothills. Higher up the slopes, cork oaks are cultivated for their valuable outer bark, which is cut only once every nine years. Forests of fast-growing eucalyptus trees supply paper manufacturing industries.

Tourism is by far the main economic activity in the Algarve nowadays. It goes hand-in-hand with construction. Since the opening of the international airport at Faro in the 1960s, there has been a vast amount of development, in some places over-development. Most lamentably, there has been some wholesale destruction of the **natural environment**.

During the chaotic, gold-rush days of the 1980s, no part of the Algarve's proud heritage and no stretch of its fabulous coastline seemed immune from developers on the rampage with their backhanders and bulldozers. The bricks and mortar brigades, aided and abetted by the seemingly insatiable demands of mass-tourism, wreaked havoc until it was realised that they were destroying the very natural beauty that tourists were seeking.

Order has been restored. Strict land usage plans and building restrictions are in place. There is now a keen awareness that the conservation of the region's fragile habitats, flora and fauna are not only compatible with sound, tourism-based economical development, but essential to it.

Barragem do Funcho

21

PEOPLE

ALGARVIOS

There are local and regional rivalries, but the Portuguese are a homogeneous and intensely patriotic people, united by a long and often turbulent history. They have absorbed successive lengthy occupations, led the world in geographical discovery and empire building, survived centuries of internal strife, revolutions and war. A people like this have depth and backbone. They are not going to wince at having to adapt to modern trends, like the European Union, the euro single currency or the challenges posed by mass tourism from abroad.

The people of the Algarve are referred to disparagingly by northern Portuguese as *Mouros* (Moors). It would be strange if, after 500 years of occupation, the Moors did not leave behind some ingrained characteristics, but what the northerners are getting at is that the people of the south are somehow different from other Portuguese. Indeed they are. The Algarve has never been a place of royal palaces or grand estates, a centre of industrial production or social sophistication.

Almost throughout their history, the Algarvios have been poor, provincial, rural and isolated. As recently as the 1960s there were very few telephones or cars in the Algarve. The road and rail links with the rest of the country were torturous. It took many hours to get to or from Lisbon and the journey almost always involved an overnight stop. The opening of Faro International Airport, in 1968, was thus a seminal event. It quickly led to mass tourism and dramatic changes to the Algarve landscape and its people.

Tourism prompted a migration from the land to urban areas, particularly the towns along the coast. The prospect of employment in tourism and associated service and construction industries also drew Portuguese people from outside the region.

An ever-growing number of foreigners from abroad, especially Britain and Germany, have come here to work, but mostly to retire. In recent years there has been a big influx from Eastern Europe, mainly as construction workers. One way and another the permanent population of the Algarve has greatly increased.

Of a total population of al-

most 10.5 million in Portugal, about 400,000 live in the Algarve. With the flood of tourists from abroad and from northern Portuguese cities, the population of the Algarve triples in July and August.

The biggest urban areas are Faro and Portimão, followed by Loulé, Albufeira and Lagos. They are all of ancient origin. In the past few decades many luxury private complexes have been developed. Some of them, like Vilamoura, are as large as small cities. Vale do Lobo, the Algarve's first major golf development, prides itself on being three times the size of Monaco.

Only 40 or 50 kilometres from the millionaire mansions of Quinta do Lago there are smallholdings that might as well be light years away. Subsistence farmers sow and reap by hand and live in stone houses in conditions reminiscent of Biblical times. Between these extremes is where you find most Algarvio families, living on wages well below the EU average, but with values and a quality of life that in many respects far exceed the EU average.

This is a family-orientated society. Family roots run deep, generations stick together and genuinely enjoy each other's company. Traditional values remain strong, though they have changed in recent years in two important respects.

Firstly, the Algarvios are no longer predominately Roman Catholic, God-fearing people; only a small proportion now regularly attend church and some of those who do prefer more modern evangelical churches.

Secondly, women have been emancipated. The joke used to be that the donkey was too small for both a man and his wife, which was why his wife walked behind. Nowadays, the person behind the wheel of the classy car passing you on the motorway is just as likely to be a woman as a man. Male chauvinism has been shattered. Portugal's universities are producing more female than male graduates and many of them move on to occupy top positions, especially in the legal and medical professions.

Portugal has no external enemies, no internal dissident groups. It is largely free from racial tension and social unrest. Violent crime is rare in the Algarve. Unfortunately, but unsurprisingly, drug-related crime has become endemic. Holidaymakers can walk the streets without fear of physical attack, but it as well to be aware that thefts from houses

and cars are not uncommon. The culprits are mostly unorganized, unimaginative and looking for cash or cameras to finance another fix.

FIRST FACES

Many of the Portuguese whom tourists are most likely to come into direct contact with understand and speak English well. On arrival a nod is all you are likely to get from the **immigration official** who examines your passport. You probably won't get even that from the **customs man.**

If you are on a package holiday, a **tour company rep** armed with a brightly coloured folder and a tally sheet will probably have a word with you once you have cleared the baggage hall. The rep is there to check your arrival and give initial advice. Detailed information and answers to your queries come after you have settled into your accommodation.

The **car hire desks** at the airport are all in a row almost in front of you as you emerge from the baggage hall. A clerk will want to see your driving licence before filling in the relevant forms, handing over the car keys and directing you to the car park directly in front of the terminal building.

Independent travellers who want information about accommodation, taxi fares, bus services and the like can get it all from the official **tourist information desk** in the arrivals' hall.

Taxis, all cream-coloured,

25

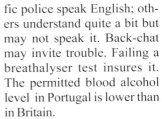

line up just outside the terminal. Algarve taxi drivers are generally honest and helpful. To avoid any confusion later, establish the fixed-price fare to your destination before you set off.

Self-drive visitors may encounter **traffic police** checkpoints. The police are usually polite but uncompromising, as strict and humourless with foreign visitors as local residents. They will want to see the car registration and insurance documents and your driving licence. Always have them with you in the car. Some traffic police speak English; others understand quite a bit but may not speak it. Back-chat may invite trouble. Failing a breathalyser test insures it. The permitted blood alcohol level in Portugal is lower than in Britain.

Nearly all **receptionists** in hotels, holiday complexes and campsites speak fluent English and some can manage German and French as well. If you are staying in an independent villa or apartment with no receptionist to turn to for advice, make sure you are able to make contact with whoever manages the property. **House managers** are on call to deal with such things as plumbing and electrical emergencies.

The duties of **maids** in self-catering villas and apartments vary. In addition to cleaning, tidying and making beds, some are supposed to wash up dishes, some are not. Some will wash and iron your clothes, but there will probably be a charge. Maids work set hours, usually on weekday mornings, but not at weekends or on public holidays.

Communicating with **bank tellers**, **post office clerks, waiters** and **shop-keepers** is generally not a problem and they are usually helpful and patient with visitors who don't know the system.

OUT & ABOUT

The Algarvios and immigrants living and working along the coast have taken the phenomenal growth in tourism in their stride and prospered. The lives of those living inland have been less affected. They have benefited from improved roads and greater demand for agricultural products, but rural friendliness and traditional ways of doing things prevail. It is in the country areas that you find what is sometimes referred to as the 'real' Algarve.

The average age inland is higher than on the coast. The standard of living is lower and the pace of life slower. Some country folk still live in simple cottage homes with no electricity or running water, supporting themselves on subsistence farming and meagre state pensions.

In summer as in winter, day as well as night, country folk keep well covered. Clothes function in the same way as thatched roofs, or like double glazing: they keep the heat out in summer and the reverse in winter. Rural Algarvios recoil at the idea of air-conditioning or central heating. If their own cottage homes have fires, they are for cooking not for warming the place up. Unnatural

temperature manipulation invites colds and other illness, they say.

Outside of tourist areas, visitors may come across unfamiliar sounds and what seems like strange or even suspicious behavior. For example, a characteristic of the Algarve countryside in September is the rattle of long poles being wielded among the branches of almond or carob trees. This is the time-honoured way of harvesting almond nuts and carob beans.

At about the same time of year, women can be seen in certain areas laying out big

27

Drying figs and carob beans

sheets of plastic beneath a certain bushy type of tree. They are collecting olives.

At almost any time during the first half of the year, men and women may be encountered snooping around in the shrubbery. They are up to nothing more sinister than gathering edible snails (*caracois* or *caracoletas*), which are considered a delicacy.

The objects you may not be able to distinguish, scattered on bamboo mats in the open-air outside cottages in August, are likely to be figs drying in the sun. Figs are a key ingredient in locally-made cakes.

It may seem strange to see women walking about with open umbrellas in summer, even though there is not a rain cloud in sight. To protect against sunburn, country-women often also wear trilby hats on top of headscarves hanging in such a way that they cover the ears and neck. If you see a person with the skin colour of a well-cooked prawn, for sure it is a foreign holidaymaker who has failed to take sensible precautions.

Flute-like notes emanating from a sort of mouth organ announce the presence of the knife-sharpening man. For small change he will hone your kitchen implements on a revolving whetstone on the back of his bike. An irritating klaxon may signal the arrival in the neighbourhood of a travelling breadman or fish-seller.

Townsfolk think nothing of cooking sardines on makeshift charcoal grills on the public pavement outside their home. And while the old boys sit on a wall chatting, the womenfolk sit in their doorways with lightening fingers busy, not with knitting, but with crochet work.

There is an unkind Portuguese joke, usually aimed at the people of the Alentejo, the province to the north of the Algarve: 'in a race between a man and a snail, who wins?' Answer: 'the man, because the snail was disqualified for making three false starts.'

Life is no more hectic in rural Algarve than it is in the Alentejo. Not many things provoke any sense of urgency. Punctuality is a foreign concept. So, most of the time, is speed. Yet all the notions of the Portuguese being a totally laid-back people change on the roads.

To watch the kamikaze behaviour of drivers is spell-binding. Portugal is reputed to have the highest road accident rate in Europe. Reckless tailgating and overtaking in dangerous situations seem almost standard, but it all seems somehow out of character. One possible explanation is that the Algarve moved too quickly from donkey power to Datsuns, from mule-carts to Mazdas, from mud lanes to motorways. It all happened within one generation.

The Algarve in some ways continues to be a sleepy backwater. Despite this, or because of it, Portugal's sunny south is also remarkably cosmopolitan, a good place to meet ordinary, decent people from all over the world.

CELEBRITIES

The rich and famous come and go without fuss in the Algarve. No one takes much notice. At the very height of his fame as one the greatest Formula One world champions of all time, Ayrton Senna could be seen jogging and walking his dogs, four adopted strays, in the streets around his home at Quinta do Lago. Sir Cliff Richard, who has had a holiday home here since 1961 and now produces the Algarve's finest wine, can sit down to a plate of chicken and chips in a local restaurant without fear of being molested. The legendary goalkeeper David Seaman once confided that the next best thing to playing for England or in a Cup Final was a quiet round of golf near his home in the utterly uncrowded western Algarve.

DISABLED

Faro airport is wheelchair friendly. If you want to be met with a wheelchair, be sure to request it in advance through a travel company. Less consideration for the special needs of the disabled is in evidence in hotels, restaurants and other places.

Wheeling Around the Algarve is a company specialising in holidays for the disabled. Their contacts: www.player.pt; info@player.pt tel. (00351) 289 393636; fax 2828 397448.

Qualified nursing care, cars with hand controls, equipment such as pool hoists, dolphin therapy and sports facilities, including horse-riding lessons specifically designed for disabled beginners, are all available in the Algarve.

WOMEN ONLY

For unaccompanied women, there are probably fewer safer streets in Europe than those in the Algarve. Women walking alone rarely have anything to fear. That said, common-sense caution should not be thrown to the wind. Hitch-hiking alone, for example, is no more advisable here than anywhere else.

Young and attractive women, especially foreign women, can expect to be given the eye much more openly in Portugal than in northern Europe. Many women find this kind of attention flattering at first, but annoying if it persists. Whistles and suggestive comments from construction sites are more common in Lisbon and the north of Portugal than the Algarve, where the local lads are more used to seeing foreigners.

Unaccompanied women need not worry about being molested in restaurants, bars or discos provided, of course, they don't invite undue attention by being excessively provocative.

MEN ONLY

Foreign men hoping to score with Portuguese women while on holiday should be wary of causing offence. Portuguese women are generally much more bound up in traditional restraints than their counterparts in northern Europe. For casual liaisons, your prospects are far better among female fellow-travellers. Of course, you can expect stiff competition from macho Portuguese guys who like foreign looks and have ready-made reputations as Latin lovers.

Homosexuality is, generally-speaking, a much more discreet and private matter than in other countries. There are few places catering exclusively or mainly for gays.

Bear in mind that relaxed attitudes in a holiday atmosphere not only encourage pleasurable promiscuity, either hetero or homosexual, but may also promote the spread of AIDS.

CHILDREN

The Portuguese are as friendly and caring towards visiting children from abroad as they are towards their own. Nowhere are children of any age shunned, and that includes restaurants and bars at night-time.

Mothers don't need to pack **baby foods**, medications, nappies and the like. These are all readily available in Algarve shops.

When the weather is good there is plenty for children to do. **Wet weather** may pose a problem, however. If visiting anytime between October and April, pack some of the children's favourite books and games. Such things in English are not easily found in the Algarve.

Indoor facilities are available for swimming (both private and public pools), bowling, squash, aerobics, table tennis, snooker, pool and – horror of horrors – visits to museums.

The **beach** is the fair-weather favourite among youngsters of all ages. No beach anywhere can be considered totally 'safe' but the dangers are minimal on popular, calm-water beaches on the south coast with a safety-flag system and lifeguards. Even good swimmers should be wary of getting out of their depth off the west coast, where the undertow is often strong.

Swimming pools are usually a child's delight, but some common sense precautions should be borne in mind:

• As parents, don't get lured into a false sense of security because a pool is fenced and access blocked by a locked gate. Children love a challenge. Fences are to be climbed and locks are sometimes carelessly left open.

• Don't assume that because children can swim well they can be left unattended without risk. A fall next to or in a pool, for example, can be fatal.

Water parks are well aware of potential hazards and specifically equipped and staffed to deal with emergencies. Entrance prices may seem steep, but they are reasonable when you consider that not only the children, but the whole family, can enjoy a full day of fun at these parks.

The very name **Zoomarine** (situated near Guia) is enough to put some animal lovers off. Stay clear if you are adamantly opposed to dolphins and

---

LITTLE ANGELS

"To the Portuguese, small children no matter how noisy and ill-behaved, are angels to be adored and worshipped, overdressed and under disciplined."

Marion Kaplan, *The Portuguese, the Land and its People.*

other acquatic creatures being kept in captivity and used to entertain. Many skeptics who visit later admit to respecting the conditions under which the animals are kept and the educational as well as amusement value of the park. Most kids love it. Apart from animal displays, there are ordinary swimming pools and other play facilities, all included in the entrance charge. Swimming in the pool alongside the dolphins is quite a bit extra.

Crazy World, near Algoz, is a mixture of animal park and fun putting course, plus bumper car, a big wheel and other fairground amusements.

Serious sport facilities and lessons for young people:

golf, especially at Parque da Floresta, west of Lagos; **tennis**, (Vale do Lobo and near Carvoeiro); **archery**, (Vilamoura); **horse-riding**, (Almancil area and many other places). The full range of **watersports** can be indulged in at many beaches along the south coast. **Game fishing** boats operate out of Vilamoura and Portimão. **Mountain bikes** can be easily hired.

Among the more passive ways of passing the time with the children: **coastal cruises**, short or long, leave from many beaches and from quaysides in the larger ports; **river cruises** start from Portimão and from Vila Real de Stº António.

CENTRAL ALGARVE

After arrival at Faro Airport, most visitors turn west and head for the hotels and tourist complexes in and around Almancil, Quarteira, Vilamoura, Albufeira, Armação de Pera, Carvoeiro, Praia da Rocha, Alvor and Lagos.

ALMANCIL is a busy commercial village on the way to the plush golf resorts of Quinta do Lago and Vale do Lobo. There is everything in the neighbourhood for the most fastidious holidaying hedonist: the finest restaurants, nightclubs, shops, cultural centres and sports facilities, all within close proximity to the region's most luxurious villas.

VILAMOURA may be a notch or two down on the luxury ladder, but it is a much larger resort, reputedly the largest private development in Europe. It has the south coast's largest marina, four

Quarteira west end

golf courses and facilities for a host of other sports, including some of the less obvious ones like clay pigeon shooting and archery.

Proud of its concern for the natural environmental, there are plenty of green spaces around the various complexes within the overall estate. The heart of the matter, though, is the marina presided over by the huge, five-star Marinotel and surrounded by all kinds of restaurants and bars.

The marina is a base for all water-sports, including game fishing, during the warmer months. Most of the game fish caught off Vilamoura are blue or mako sharks. They are tagged and returned to the sea. Marlin are also sought, but much less often encountered.

Two establishments of contrasting character near the marina are the Cerro da Vila Roman ruins and the Vilamoura Casino. The latter is not quite up to Las Vegas standards, but it is perfectly adequate to while away time and money on one-armed bandits and roulette.

Just to the east of Vilamoura is what guidebooks used to describe as the 'quaint little fishing village' of **QUARTEIRA**. It has changed a lot in recent years and is now an assertive, relatively high-rise seaside town brimming with apartments. It's a bit bleak in winter, but in summer the area is full of package holiday tourists from abroad, as well as Portuguese visitors from Lisbon and the other cities to the north.

Quarteira's transformation from small community innocence to brassy holiday destination inevitably involved a physical and social upheaval.

In being built up, it was seriously messed up, but in recent years there has been a concerted effort to tidy up.

As a small example of Quarteira's mellowing maturity, halfway along its palm-fringed beachfront promenade, next to the tourist information office, there is a municipal art gallery.

The long, long beach is punctuated at intervals by breakwaters to help control the natural erosion of the coastline. A new harbour has been built for the local fishing fleet, which has not only survived but also profited from the transformation from 'quaintness'.

As a holiday destination, **ALBUFEIRA**, is the sort of place you either love or hate. A great number of people of all ages love it because it bubbles and froths. Curiously, many elderly people seem to feel as much at home here as teenagers and couples with young families.

The town continues to spread out rather than up. On either side of its small, historic centre, the town extends all the way to Olhos d'Água and Falésia in the east, and beyond the new marina to Galé and Salgados in the west. The whole area – greater Albufeira, we might call it – has very little to do with normal workaday Portugal. It is the most tourist intensive place in the country.

Albufeira existed at least 2,000 years ago as a small Roman settlement called Baltrum. Eight centuries later the Moors renamed it Al-Buhera,

Albufeira beach

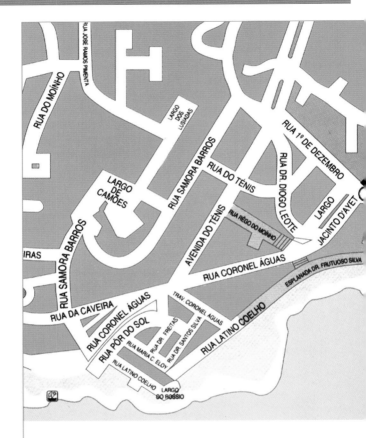

**Central
Albufeira
Plan**

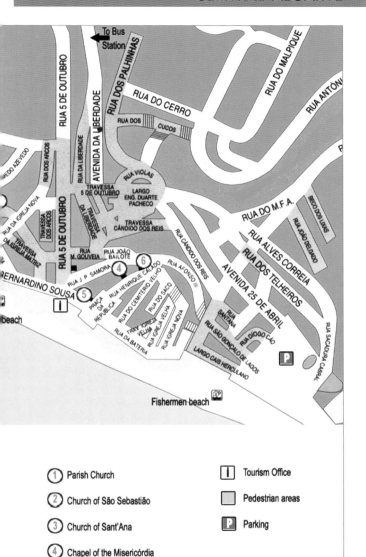

1. Parish Church
2. Church of São Sebastião
3. Church of Sant'Ana
4. Chapel of the Misericórdia
5. Clock Tower
6. Castle Walls

Tourism Office
Pedestrian areas
Parking

meaning in Arabic 'castle by the sea'. The Moors turned it into a prosperous port trading with North Africa. All was well until an army of Knights of Santiago captured the town in 1250. They returned it to Portuguese control but, in doing so, extinguished its trade links with North Africa. Thereafter, Albufeira fell upon hard times that lasted for hundreds of years.

It suffered a succession of earthquakes in 1719, 1722 and then, worst of all, in 1755. Having been rebuilt, Albufeira was besieged then burnt to the ground during a civil war in 1833. Prosperity only returned with the tourist boom that got underway in the 1970s. Tourism is what Albufeira is now all about.

Some of the charm of the old town is still there. It is to be found in the labyrinth of narrow streets, whitewashed houses, cafés and shops stacked up on the hillside above the central square, Largo Eng. Duarte Pacheco.

Streets off the square lead to one of the two central beaches. The first is known as Fishermen's beach and is shared without a shred of self-consciousness by topless sun-bathers and leather-skinned men of the sea, who are far too busy mending their nets to notice the bare boobs bobbing about their boats.

The other beach is at the end of a tunnel through the rock face, next to the tourist information office.

The street affectionately

Salgados beach

known as 'the strip' is located to the east of the old town, in a neighbourhood called Areias de São João. The strip stretches from the Montechoro Hotel, past scores of cafés, restaurants and bars, down to a busy beach called Praia da Oura. Many cafés and bars along here advertise 'full English breakfasts' to help overcome the hangovers caused by imbibing on the strip well into the wee hours the night before.

There is an abundance of holiday accommodation in Albufeira and the broad area around it. The accommodation ranges from good hotels to a good campsite but, without advance booking, you may find it difficult to get your head down anywhere in summer.

To the west of Albufeira and set back a little from the coast, the village of **GUIA** was, for many years, best known locally for chicken piri-piri restaurants. Now it is becoming famous internationally for its wine. The Algarve had never managed to produce wine of real quality until singer Sir Cliff Richard launched his Vida Nova red in 2001.

The Vida Nova grapes are grown in Sir Cliff's own vineyard and those of Guia neighbours. Visitors are welcome, by appointment, to tour the modern Quinta do Miradouro winery where Vida Nova is produced.

South of Guia, the sand dunes and beaches of Galé and Salgados roll westward to

Armação de Pera beach
Sra. da Rocha chapel

join with the long beach and low cliffs in front of **ARMAÇÃO DE PERA.** Since the 1970s, developers have succeeded in spoiling Armação de Pera where centuries of pirate raiders from the sea failed. In days of yore, this was a settlement of smallholdings and fishermen's huts huddled around a protective fort, remnants of which still survive on the seafront. It became a favourite weekend retreat for farmers and their families from the Silves area. When it started to catch on among holidaymakers from Lisbon and abroad, developers fell over themselves to erect eye-sore apartment blocks.

That said, Armação is not all bad. The best thing about it is undoubtedly the beach. It stretches for miles and becomes progressively less crowded as you walk away from the built-up area. The town's two best-known landmarks are its first hotel, the Garbe, and an old mansion with palm trees in the garden that juts out over the beach.

Outside of the town on the west side, there is a series of lovely little coves and two of the Algarve's finest luxury hotel complexes, Vila Lara and Vila Vita Parc. By contrast, fishermen long ago built a little

Carvoeiro

chapel, on the site where an apparition of the Virgin Mary is said to have appeared, high on a sheer headland separating the twin beaches at Senhora da Rocha.

Back at the main road (EN125), the village of **PORCHES** has two potteries, Porches Pottery and Olaria Pequena, which produce original hand-painted pieces, far superior to anything on offer in the many *artesanato* handicraft shops along the way.

LAGOA is the Algarve's biggest producer of wine. Most of it is strong, rough and ready table wine, both red and white. The co-operative winery, on the turn-off to Carvoeiro, also produces a little fortified wine. All of it comes from grapes grown over a wide area around the town.

CARVOEIRO is a much more modest place than you might imagine, from the prominence it is given in holiday brochures and accommodation advertisements in British national newspapers. Apart from its far-flung reputation, it has managed to keep a low profile, having spread sideways rather than upwards. Suburbs of good quality villas, most of them with private pools, have been built to the east and west of the village. There are a few good hotels in the vicinity (Almansor and Carvoeiro Sol). The place with the best view of all is Casa Baselli, a small B&B guesthouse right above Carvoeiro beach.

There are a few other guesthouses and hotels, but this is mainly holiday villaland, extremely active in summer. By day, visitors lounge around their private pools or languish on one of the several lovely beaches in the neighbourhood. (The beaches, east to west, are: Albandeira, Marinha, Benagil, Carvalho, Centianes, Carvoeiro, Paraíso). In the evening, nearly everyone staying in supposedly self-catering villas or apartments converges on Carvoeiro's many restaurants.

Like most other holiday villages in the Algarve, the shutters come down in Carvoeiro with the first signs of winter in early November. Much of the neighbourhood goes into hibernation until Easter.

There are two notable areas of continued activity throughout the winter months and they are on the golf courses to the west and east of the village. To the west are Pestana's Pinta and Gramacho courses, each 18 holes; to the east is the nine-hole Vale do Milho course, a good test of a golfer's short game.

No village along the Barlavento coast is totally untouched by tourism, but **FERRAGUDO** is far less affected than most. Sitting within the eastern breakwater at the mouth of the river Arade, it maintains a quiet air of unpretentiousness. It looks unenviously across the river to Portimão and Praia da Rocha. Around sunset, the view from the Casabela Hotel, near Ferragudo, is gloriously romantic.

There is a limited but interesting choice of local beaches: Carneios and Pintadinho are small and both front on to the sea; Cais is

Arade river from Ferragudo

Old bridge into Portimão

very small and is right next to the eastern breakwater at the mouth of the Arade river; Praia Grande, as its name suggests, is the biggest of the beaches, but it fronts on to the river estuary, not the open sea, which has both advantages and disadvantages.

PORTIMÃO is the Algarve's second most important commercial town, after Faro, and its second largest port, after Olhão. It is a town of great antiquity but you wouldn't know it. The oldest building is its much renovated parish church. It contains 17th and 18th-century tiles, but the only really old bit is the 14th-century portal. Portimão today is mostly about shopping and eating sardines by the riverside. One of the best shopping streets is Rua do Comércio, a pedes-

trian mall which begins at the square near the parish church in the highest part of town. The river is, and always has been, the town's life-blood. The fishing fleet ties up in the

Portimão parish church

45

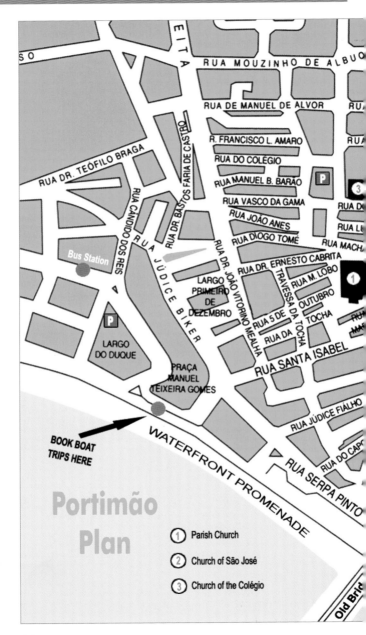

BOOK BOAT TRIPS HERE

Portimão Plan

① Parish Church

② Church of São José

③ Church of the Colégio

46

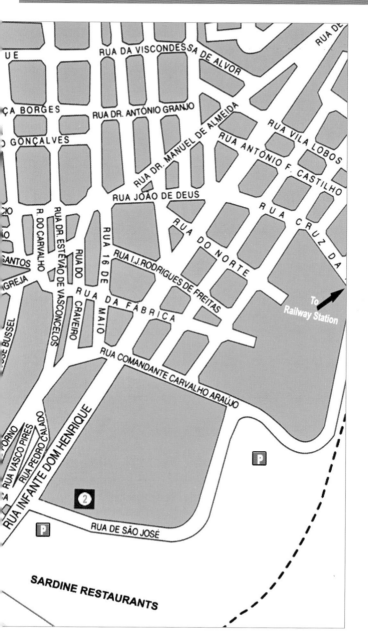

Praia da Rocha

harbour on the far bank. Some of its catch is brought over to Portimão's most popular open-air eating area, on the quayside on the upstream side of the old iron bridge. There are more restaurants, in converted boat houses, in a little square beneath the town end of the bridge.

If you want to try catching your own fish on rod and line, the Portimão quayside is one of the main departure points in the Algarve for coarse and game fishing boats. Also tied up along the same quayside, various other types of craft carry billboards offering coastal sightseeing cruises or trips up the river Arade to the historic town of Silves.

The Praça Teixeira Gomes, with its fountain and open-air cafés next to the waterfront, is the main meeting place during

the summer months. Nearby, a smaller square, Lago 1 de Dezembro, is notable for its 19th-century tiled panels depicting 10 of the greatest events in Portuguese history.

PRAIA DA ROCHA is Portimão's seafront suburb. Immensely popular in summer, especially among the young, it was the first place to be developed as a resort in the Algarve. Many would say it has now gone over the top, for it is dominated by row upon row of holiday apartment blocks rising 15 storeys or more above a plethora of cafés, bars and restaurants overlooking a vast beach.

At the eastern end of the beach, guarding the entrance to the river, stands the remnants of the Fortress of Santa Catarina, built between 1521 and 1557. It looks down on a marina on one side and the beach on another. The main beach here is actually composed of sand dredged from the riverbed to make the Arade deeper and more navigable.

At the western end of the main beach, a tunnel called the Buraco da Avó (Grandmother's Hole) connects with a chain of narrower, rockier but delightful beaches sheltering under low cliffs.

The beachfront road runs westward to a substantial spread of sand at Praia de Vau. The cliffs then temporarily peter out and the road curls inland a little, eventually emerging at the river-mouth village of **ALVOR**.

We are now getting into territory beloved by the legendary golfer, Sir Henry Cotton, who lived in this part of the Algarve for many years and is buried, next to his wife, in the village of Mexilhoeira Grande. The 18-hole Alto Golf course between Praia de Vau and Alvor was the last course he designed. His first course, the venerable Penina, which is situated inland, next to the EN125, was opened in 1965.

Tucked away amidst golf courses, hotels, holiday developments and leisure facilities, including an aerodrome for light aircraft, is the old village of Alvor with narrow streets running down to the water's edge, where the fishing boats are moored. Beyond the harbour is another of those vast sandy beaches.

Alvor has made a couple of footnotes in history. Dom João II, the so-called "Perfect Prince" who went on to rule during the Age of Discovery as one of Portugal's greatest kings, died here of dropsy in 1495. Five centuries later, in 1975, an international agreement granting independence to the African state of Angola was negotiated in little old Alvor.

It had a castle once upon a time, but almost nothing of it remains. In the nearby parish church, the oldest intact architectural feature is the main doorway, a fine example of the ornate Manueline Gothic style, devised and made popular during the reign of João II's successor, Manuel I.

Alvor church looks out over an estuary, the Quinta da Rocha headland, and the eastern side of the bay that sweeps all the way around to Lagos.

The estuary is excellent for shellfish and birdwatching, but it rules out a direct route along the coast to Lagos. The only way is to return to the main EN125 road or the A22 motorway.

WESTERN ALGARVE

LAGOS is the most historically interesting town in the Algarve. It is also one of the most relaxed. Its fame derives from its association with Portugal's 14th and 15th century Age of Discovery. It was here that Henry the Navigator had his vessels built and supplied for the voyages of exploration to the Atlantic islands of Madeira and the Azores, and down the coast of West Africa to Guinea.

One of the most formidable milestones in the quest for a sea passage to the Orient was Cape Bojador, a headland on the bulge of Africa, which struck terror in the hearts of medieval seafarers. It was an awesome promontory, not only because it was veiled in myths and legends, but also because of very real and treacherous winds and currents that made it almost impossible to round.

The first European captain to achieve this feat was Gil Eanes, Lagos' most famous son. He did so in 1495 after many others before him had failed. It was one of the greatest achievements of Henry's lifetime, because it led to the opening of the sea route past the Cape of Good Hope to India.

Both Henry and Gil Eanes are commemorated with statues in Lagos on the town side of the avenue next to the harbour (Avenida dos Descobrimentos). From his pedestal, Henry, astrolabe in hand, looks over the Praça da República.

Gil Eanes, looking suitably pleased with himself, is in front of the town walls a little farther along to the west.

The town's third figurative statue is of the boy-king, Sebastian (pictured page 52), who brought about the demise of the Aviz dynasty in the 16th century by sailing from Lagos to a disastrous defeat against a Moorish army in Morocco. Although the subject of many a rude remark, Sebastian's statue in Largo Gil Eanes is by the respected Portuguese sculptor, João Cutileiro.

Just before they set sail Sebastian, aged 21, is said to have given his troops a pep talk from a window in a corner of what was then the Algarve Governor's palace. It is a small, rather florid Manuline-style window, fairly high on the wall to the left of Henry's statue.

Like Sebastian's window, Henry's slave market (*Mercado dos escravis*), in another corner of the Praça da República, looks ordinary nowadays. The first market in Portugal to publicly auction slaves brought back from Africa by Henry's explorers and traders is now a little gallery used to exhibit works by local artists.

The town walls are well renovated but still suggest a town of ancient origins. The Carthaginians had a fortified trading settlement here. It was taken over, enlarged and further fortified by the Romans. They called it Lacobriga.

The Moors developed Lacobriga into an important

Praça da República, Lagos

Lagos Marina

port trading with North Africa from the 8th century until Christian Portuguese finally penetrated the walls in 1249.

The town walls came tumbling down along with nearly all the buildings within them during the earthquake of 1755. Among the buildings since rebuilt are the Church of Santa Maria and the regimental storehouse adjacent to it. Both are in the Praça da República, behind Henry's statue.

Behind them again, a little further inside the town, is Lagos' most extraordinary building, the 'golden' Church of Santo António next to the local museum. The interior, almost all of it, is a brilliant example of the art of gilded wood carving.

Lagos' hey-day was from 1420 to 1460 when Henry prayed in its churches and strode its quaysides. It remained a busy commercial port until Sebastian's Morocco adventure. From then on, it went into decline and was reduced to a simple fishing port.

Because of its history, its bayside location and its proximity to spectacular beaches, it became a natural attraction once tourism got underway in the second half of the 20th century. In keeping with its maritime past, the latest addition to Lagos' attractions is a yacht marina at the most sheltered end of the harbour. It is the home port of the *Boa Esperança*, a replica of the kind of vessel commissioned by Henry in the 15th century.

Lagos may not be among Portugal's most beautiful towns, but its faded glory, its

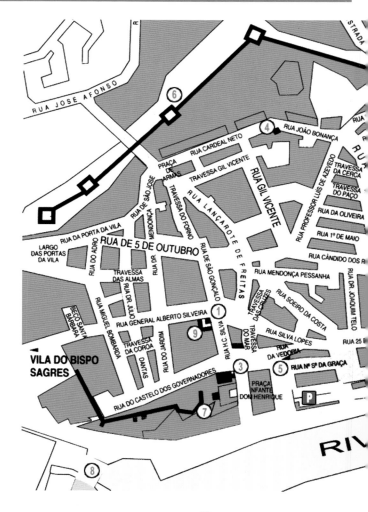

Lagos Plan

1. Church of Santo António
2. Church of São Sebastião
3. Church of Santa Maria or Misericórdia
4. Church of Nossa Senhora do Carmo
5. Slave Market

(6) Fortifications

(7) Castle of the Governors

(8) Fort Ponta da Bandeira

(9) Municipal Museum

[i] Tourism Office

Luz Black Rock

relaxed atmosphere and quiet charm make it one of the most appealing to visitors from abroad. The best places to sit and watch people go by are at the open-air cafés in Praça da República or on the walkway on the harbour side of the Avenida. The best selection of restaurants is concentrated in the pedestrian-only Rua 25 de Abril.

There is a beach called Batata nestling next to the little fort guarding the entrance to the harbour. The main beaches, however, are on either side of the town. Meia Praia is the long strand that sweeps around from Alvor on the east side. Dona Ana to the west is more attractive. Beyond Dona Ana lie the beach at Porto do Mós and the rugged headland of Ponta da Piedade.

The holiday scene in Lagos is hardly hectic, but it is lively compared with everything to the west of it. **PRAIA DA LUZ** has rapidly expanded in recent years from one of those 'quaint little fishing villages' into a rather cluttered holiday destination. Its main appeal is its beach and best-known landmark, the so-called 'Black Rock' that beckons to be climbed.

BURGAU and **SALEMA** are smaller and more innocent versions of Luz, but they could yet go the same way. Two enduring features of Burgau, which still almost fit into the category of 'quaint', are the splendidly and slightly precariously located bar on the beach, and the Casa Grande guest house, said to have friendly ghosts in permanent residence.

The southwest coast has a few other beaches of particular appeal to adventurous visitors. Boca do Rio, between Burgau and Salema and overlooked by the ruins of a 16th century fort at Ponta da Almádena, has a sunken wreck offshore which attracts scuba divers and snorkellers. It is the wreck of an 18th century French warship, L'Ócean. Surfers and windsurfers, meanwhile, make their way to Ingrina and Zavial, a narrow pair of beaches reached by a road from the village of Raposeira.

Golfers can play the Algarve's most westerly course at Parque da Floresta, just past the village of Budens. Between there and Raposeira, on the right going west, history buffs will want to call in on one of the region's oldest places of worship, the starkly simple Chapel of Nossa Senhora de Guadalupe, possibly built in th 13th century. Henry the Navigator almost certainly worshiped there and he is thought to have owned the lands around the chapel. He also had a house in Raposeira.

Pre-history buffs can wander among a scattering of megalithic stones in a marked walk

Guadalupe church

through the grain fields of Monte dos Amantes, a short distance out of Vila do Bispo on a minor road on the right (not the main road) towards Sagres.

SAGRES is the big magnet in this part of the Algarve. People from all over the world are drawn here because of its historical connections, or simply because of its geographical position in the extreme southwest corner of Europe. Henry the Navigator built a village and named it after himself at, or near, the present-day village. Vila do Infante, as it was

Salema beach

called, is thought to have been the location of a school of navigation which attracted some of the best brains in cartography and nautical sciences during Henry's lifetime.

It is tempting to think of the 'school' as a medieval research centre, a forerunner of NASA headquarters. It is reasonable to speculate that it may have been located within the fortress ramparts guarding Sagres headland. In truth, though, almost nothing is known for sure about the school's precise composition or location.

The only 15th century building still standing within the ramparts is the little Church of Nossa Senhora da Graça.

The origin and purpose of the circular *rosa dos ventos* (compass of the winds) is unclear, but it does not date from Henry's time. The largest and most recently constructed building within the *fortaleza* is an exhibition centre, a monument to bad taste and to historical and environmental insensitivity. There are some who believe it deserves no better a fate than that which befell Henry's Vila do Infante in about 1587: it was demolished, by Sir Francis Drake.

As you admire the rugged seascape while walking around the headland path within the fortress walls, you can imagine the dramatic mood changes that nature sometimes conjures here. You will probably see men with long rods casting a very long way down into the turbulent waters. You may marvel at their head for heights. If they seem in danger of falling from their cliff-ledge perches,

Sagres headland

Cape St Vincent

indeed they are. Occasionally they do.

Next to the unmanned lighthouse, on the point of the Sagres headland, there is a good example of a blowhole - a natural, vertical vent rising from the roof of a cavern in the base of the cliff, right up to the cliff top. When the sea is rough, the waves pound into the cavern, whooshing air upwards and then sucking it back down again.

Although Sagres is a 'must' for all visitors to the Algarve, the village itself is a bit of a shambles. It is a hotchpotch of houses and apartments with a few hotels and a road that winds down to a sheltered fishing harbour. Some of best bedroom views are to be had from the Pousada do Infante, one of a chain of Portuguese state-run hotels. Travellers on a tight budget may have to settle for a modest room in a private house or stay in the local campsite.

The closest thing to a village centre is the little square, Praça da República, where backpackers of many nationalities meet and swap notes over beer outside the Café Conchinha by day, and inside bars such as the Last Chance Saloon in the evening.

Just as everyone who comes to Sagres visits the fortress (at a small entrance fee), they also make the 6km trip along the road to the **CAPE ST VINCENT** lighthouse (the grounds of which are open to visitors at no charge). It is one of the most famous lighthouses in the world and has the second most powerful beam in Europe. It keeps vigil over extremely busy shipping lanes between the Suez Canal and the Mediterranean, North America and northern Europe.

There is a loose arrangement whereby lighthouse keepers take small parties of visitors up to the 1,000-watt bulbs and prisms at the top of the tower. The steps are steep, of course. There are no set times and no set charge. A small tip is in order.

There are four excellent beaches in the Sagres-Cape St Vincent area: Martinhal, Mareta, Tonel and Beliche. Your choice may depend on which way the wind is blowing. Martinhal and Mareta are open to southeasterly winds. Tonel and Beliche are more exposed to southwesterlies.

Wind direction plays an important part in bird migration, for which Sagres and Cape St Vincent are renowned among ornithologists. North and west winds in autumn often produce big passages of gannets, Cory's Shearwaters and other oceanic species. East or southeast winds are better for lands birds, most notably storks and birds of prey.

The **WEST COAST** of the Algarve is spectacularly beautiful and relatively undeveloped compared to the south coast. It is lightly populated in scattered villages and hamlets by hardy folks, most of whom make their living by farming or fishing. The trappings of tourism are minimal. Vast and uncrowded beaches are an attraction only to the more intrepid of tourists.

Access to the west coast is on the EN125 from Lagos to Vila do Bispo. At Vila do Bispo a road (EN 262) branches north to Aljezur and beyond. Aljezur may also be reached more directly by continuing on from the end of the A22 motorway, or from Monchique on the EN267.

Going north from **VILA DO BISPO**, with an eerie wind farm on the right, the first significant village you reach is **CARRAPATEIRA.** Having passed through pleasant countryside, some of it farmed, some of it wooded, a signpost at Carrapateira invites you to turn off to the Sitio do Rio restaurant and a *praia*. Some praia! A horseshoe-shaped track, which starts and finishes at Carrapateira, leads first to Bordeira beach and then on around for several kilometers to Amado beach (right). For once, the word 'breathtaking' is not an over-the-top cliché. Go see this stretch of coastline for yourself. You'll never forget it.

ALJEZUR is dominated by the ruins of a Moorish fort. Head straight for the fort at the top of the hill. From there, you will get a clear idea of the lie of the land. Aljezur can be seen to be a village in two halves. The original half clings close to the hillside. The stream at

Above: Arrifana   *Right: Odeceixe*

its base used to be infested with mosquitoes which spread malaria, once a killer disease in the Algarve, as it still is in parts of Africa. To encourage villagers to move away from the dangers of the stream, Bishop Francisco Gomes of Faro in the mid 18th century commissioned the building of a church on the far side of the fertile river valley. Many parishioners took the hint.

Just south of Aljezur, a signposted turn-off leads to a fork: the left goes to the fishing village of **ARRIFANA**; the right will eventually take you to Arrifana too, but via the beach at Monte Clérigo with its knot of holiday chalets.

Perhaps the most spectacular of the easily reached west coast beaches is Praia da Amoreira. It is signposted just north of Aljezur. The turnoff is paved all the way and it runs for several kilometres along the Aljezur river valley to terminate at the aptly named Paraíso do Mar (Paradise of the Sea) bar-restaurant.

The Algarve's most northerly beach is reached by driving through the village of **ODECEIXE**, 16km north of Aljezur. The beach is at the mouth of the Odeceixe river which separates the Algarve from the province of Alentejo.

EASTERN ALGARVE

FARO is the administrative capital of the Algarve. Let's call it a 'city' by virtue of its cathedral, but it is really only a modest provincial town in size. It is not a resort town. That's not to say it is without interest to visitors.

The most interesting part is the old, walled quarter right in the heart of the city. It is only about seven kilometers from the airport and passengers often get a low-level aerial glimpse of it as they come into land.

To get to the old town by road, follow the *centro* signs to the Praça D. Francisco Gomes, which is next to the harbour and the Manuel Bivar gardens. At the far end of the gardens, next to the tourist information office, stands the Arco da Vila (literally 'archway of the town'). Walk through (cars are restricted) and you are soon in a 16th to 18th century setting.

The small Cathedral in the Largo de Sé actually dates from the mid 13th-century and was probably built on the site of a Moorish mosque. It has been much rebuilt and restored, of course. The fine old buildings on the perimeter of the square include an 18th-century bishop's palace and the current town hall. The

statue in the square is that of Bishop Francisco Gomes, who co-ordinated the rebuilding of Faro after it was destroyed by the great earthquake of 1755.

A short walk away, but still within the walled town, is a smaller square with a grander statue, that of Dom Afonso III who conquered the last strongholds of the Moors in Portugal in the 13th century. He is positioned in front of the former Convent of Nossa Senhora da Assunção, now Faro's Archaeological and Lapidary Museum, which is full of fascinating artefacts from prehistoric to modern times.

Faro has two other museums. The Ethnological Museum gives an insight into the traditional lifestyles of the region. The Maritime Museum has lots of models, including one of Vasco da Gama's ships, *São Gabriel*, and an elaborate *armação* trap of the type formerly used to capture shoals of tuna.

The most lavishly adorned of Faro churches is that of Nossa Senhora do Carmo. It is also the spookiest. It has a bone chapel with the skeletal remains of 1,245 former monks. An inscription over the doorway translates to: "Stop here and think of the fate that will befall you."

Faro Plan

1. Cathedral
2. Carmo Church
■ Churches, chapels & museums
□ Old City
P Parking

Olhão Market

OLHÃO is the Algarve's main fishing port. It looks tatty from the main road from Faro, but it is much more interesting on the waterfront side of town. Follow the signs to the *porto* to see a colourful array of working boats. Carry on around to the municipal market (*mercado*) set in gardens, next to a broad promenade overlooking the lagoon waters of the Ria Formosa nature reserve.

The market is housed in twin buildings of mock-Moorish design. One half is devoted to seafood and has the best selection of any market in the Algarve.

From a quayside within a few minutes walk of the market, ferryboats regularly come and go to three of the **RIA FORMOSA ISLANDS** on the outer edge of the nature reserve. The main attraction of the islands are beaches of fine, white sand that disappear off into the distance. Even if the ferryboats are packed, as they usually are in summer, rest assured you will have ample elbowroom wherever you choose to lay out your towel.

Considering that the islands consist of almost nothing other than sand, a remarkable abundance of vegetation flourishes. On the island of Armona, for example, there are some large trees and even some small, well-manicured lawns. Armona has a substantial village of assorted bungalows, some basic, some quite plush. They are strung out on either side of a pathway from the harbour jetty, on the inner side of the island, to the ocean beach on the outer.

It's a 15-minute ferry ride from Olhão and then a 15-minute walk from one side of Armona to the other, with cafés in the middle as well as at either end.

The islands of Culatra and Farol merge as one at high tide. Ferries from Olhão call into both. First stop Culatra (30 minutes) has a fishing community complete with a small church and a school. The more attractive and slightly less developed option is second stop Farol, a 45-minute trip. As its name im-plies, the most conspicuous landmark on Farol is its light-house.

The most remote of the Ria Formosa islands is the unin-habited and aptly named Ilha Deserta, which can only be reached by ferry from Faro from June to September. It, too, has an ocean beach that stretches for miles. This is the best get-away island of all, not only for those who want maxi-mum sunbathing solitude, but also for those who enjoy beach and dune walking, or whose interests include botany and bird watching.

FUZETA, the next place on the mainland along the coast, is a fishing village, a miniature of Olhão. It is popular

RIA FORMOSA NATURE RESERVE

The Ria Formosa reserve is an extensive wetlands area stretching from Quinta do Lago to Manta Rota. It is a haven for shore birds at all times of the year. Some species breed, others only spend winter here. Large numbers drop by to feed and rest on their way between Europe and Africa during the spring and autumn migration periods.

The habitats are varied: salt pans, mud flats and salt marshes along the coast; the low, outer islands shelter shallow lagoon waters strewn with islets and sandbars.

One of the most easily recognizable species characteris-tic of the salt pans is the Black-winged Stilt. Many other species of wading birds are to be seen on the mud flats and marshes. An endangered species, the Little Tern, nests on the islands and the greatest care must be taken to avoid disturbing them during the breeding season.

among local windsurfers. **MONCARAPACHO** a few kilometres inland, in the heart of a fertile and well-watered area, produces oranges, lemons, and other fruits. There is a cultural gem here: the little Church of Santo Cristo and its adjoining museum. The tiles covering most of the church are 17th century. They are unusual in that, rather than depicting Biblical scenes, they are geometrically patterned in Arab style. Also, they have bright yellow colouration in addition to the more usual blue and white. The most interesting of three 17th-century carved wooden figures is a rare depiction of Christ sitting, rather than standing or nailed to the cross.

Next door to the church there is a treasure trove of artefacts ranging from the Stone Age through Roman, Visigothic and Moorish periods to a remarkable display of 18th century nativity figurines. Everything in the museum was collected by a local priest.

Back on the EN125 running parallel to the coast, you would probably drive straight through the village of **LUZ DE TAVIRA** without noticing it, were it not for its imposing parish church. The side doorway facing the main road is 16th century Manueline, quite distinct from the more recent front doorway, which is in the renaissance style.

SANTA LUZIA, a coastal village near the holiday com-

Armona Island

Tavira waterfront

plex of Pedras d'el Rei, specializes in catching octopus, as can be seen from the earthenware pots often stacked in piles along the waterfront. When laid on the sandy seabed, instinctively inquisitive octopuses can't resist crawling into them, but they usually can't find their way out.

What most visitors to Pedras d'el Rei find irresistible is Barril beach, on the outer edge of the 14km long sandbar known as Ilha de Tavira. It is quite a long hike on foot to Barril, but there is an easier option: after crossing a causeway, take a ride on the miniature train that trundles back and forth to the beach. A remarkable feature of Barril, found nowhere else in the Algarve, is what is sometimes referred to as an anchor 'cemetery'. Strangely lined up on the dunes are hundreds of large, rusting anchors, once used to keep nets in place to catch the shoals of migrating tuna fish.

TAVIRA was the tuna canning capital of the Algarve until the shoals changed their migration route and decided to keep well away from the Algarve's south coast. One of the old canneries has been converted into a comfortable hotel, the Vila Galé Albacora.

Tavira pyramid-shaped rooftops

It has a small museum dedicated to the former tuna fishing industry.

The town of Tavira is bisected by a placid river, the Gilão, which is spanned by several bridges, the oldest being of Roman origin. The main square (Praça da República), and adjoining gardens close to the Roman bridge, is the picturesque heart of Tavira.

It is an easy climb from opposite the town hall in the square, up some steps and a narrow street, to the town's highest point, on which stands the old castle battlements and the Church of Santa Maria do Castelo.

It was here that the Moors surrendered to the Christian forces of Dom Paia Pires Correia in 1242. The original mosque on the site was replaced with the present-day church and it was here that Correia was buried.

While the Church of Santa Maria do Castelo is the most prominent of Tavira's places of worship, there are many others – more, in fact, than in Faro or any other town in the Algarve. Most are no longer used for services because of crumbling structures and dwindling congregations. For the visitor interested in ecclesiastical architecture, the most ornate is the Carmo church on the opposite side of the river. The interior is a good example of baroque gone barmy.

Next to the hilltop Church of Santa Maria do Castelo, the battlements of the gardened castle offer a fine view over the 18th century, pyramid-shaped rooftops that are so characteristic of Tavira. In the middle distance, beyond the roofs, there are extensive salt pans. Beyond that are the lagoon waters of the Ria Formosa and the eastern end of Ilha de Tavira.

Ferryboats service Ilha de Tavira from Quatro Àguas, 2km from the town centre. It is a short trip to the island and the ferries run all year, most frequently (8am until late at night) in summer. From the beginning of July to mid-September, island ferries also operate from Tavira town harbour.

The Algarve has plenty of one-horse towns, but **CACELA VELHA** is no more than a one-donkey hamlet. Yet it merits a glorious footnote in history because it was here,

SALT PRODUCTION

Whether for use in cooking, preserving, pickling or industrial manufacturing, salt is naturally obtained either by mining land deposits or extracting it from the sea. The second method has been used in the Algarve, especially around Portimão, Tavira and Castro Marim, at least since Roman times.

From late March to early October, controlled flows of seawater are passed slowly through shallow, flat-bottomed ponds or 'pans', some the size of football fields. Impurities, such as sand and silt, drop to the bottom and the salt content becomes increasingly concentrated as the water slowly circulates, propelled only by gravitation and the artful manipulation of sluice gates. After several weeks, depending on the weather, concentrated brine is admitted to relatively small crystallizing pans at the end of the system. After a week or two under the full glare of the summer sun, all of the water in these pans evaporates leaving only a whitish sludge that is then raked into heaps for drying and collection.

Cacela Velha fort

in June 1833, that the English Admiral Charles Napier, known to many of his compatriots as 'Mad Charley', put 2,500 Portuguese troops ashore during Portugal's long and rather complicated War of the Two Brothers.

The only remnant of war in Cacela Velha today is a little fort, now converted to a police station, with a peaceful, panoramic view over a lagoon and one of the Algarve's longest uninterrupted stretches of sand: it starts at Cabanas and disappears into the distance towards Monte Gordo. This seamless beach of amazing proportions changes names at various signposted access points along the EN 125:

Manta Rota, Alagoas and Praia Verde all boast big expanses of sand with various tourist facilities. **MONTE GORDO,** however, is a fully fledged resort, complete with a casino. It is full of Dutch long-stay visitors during the winter months and heavily populated in summer by holidaymakers from Lisbon, Oporto, Britain, Germany and Spain.

CASTRO MARIM provides a stark contrast to Monte Gordo. Today it is a dozy inland village, but for many centuries it held a position of key importance in the life of the Algarve. It nestles between two hills, each with a fortress on top. Even though the hills are low, the fortresses have commanding views over the broad estuary of the river Guadiana, which marks the boundary between the Algarve and the Spanish province of Andalusia.

This location made Castro Marim of strategic importance in Roman times, much more so in the Middle Ages and particularly so after the Christian reconquest. Long after the Moors had been expelled from the Algarve, they remained in power in parts of southern Spain. The Spanish kingdom of Castile was an added, on-going threat and so the Portuguese were glad of the Guadiana because it acted as a natural buffer to would-be invaders.

The larger of the fortresses is referred to as Castro Marim Castle and it is possible to drive right up to the front doorway. It is all in a bad state of disrepair and disintegration, but it is possible to discern a castle within a castle. The square core of the fortifications has a conical tower at each corner of the battlements. In the 15th century this was the headquarters of an organization called the Order of Christ, a Portuguese military-religious order that succeeded the Knights Templar. Henry the Navigator was a grand master.

In later years the castle was greatly expanded to the full di-

Castro Marim castle

mensions on view today. In the 17th century, after Portugal regained its independence from 60 years of Spanish annexation, the castle was augmented by the Fort of São Sebastião on the opposite hill.

Plenty of people visit the castle, but few bother to go to the fort. Even the resident ghost in the ruins of São Sebastião (a Moorish child, it is said) seems to have given up making occasional nightly appearances.

Down river from Castro Marim, **VILA REAL DE SANTO ANTÓNIO** has probably existed as a settlement for thousands of years because of its sheltered position just inside the mouth of the Guadiana. As early as 600BC, the Phoenicians from the eastern Mediterranean were trading well beyond the fabled 'Pillars of Hercules' on either side of the Straits of Gibraltar. Their commercial sea routes, trading posts and colonies throughout the Mediterranean and on the Atlantic coasts of Western Europe were later taken over by the Carthaginians. Both peoples must have had some form of settlement at Vila Real de Santo António, though not with that name of course.

Meaning 'royal town of Saint Anthony', the Vila Real you see today was custom designed and built in the 18th century as a model fishing port with its streets all laid out in a north-south, east-west grid.

The main square bears the name of the man who requisitioned the town, the Marques of Pombal. He was the dynamic prime minister who led Portugal from the ashes of the Great Lisbon Earthquake of 1755.

The town's name is often abbreviated to Vila Real, though it is not to be confused with the industrial metropolis of that name in the northeast of Portugal. The Algarve's Vila Real is a busy little commercial town as well as a fishing port. Its shops have always attracted bargain hunters from across the border, but non-Spanish visitors, unused to border-town trading practises, should check prices with care.

Vila Real is the end of the line – or the start of it – for travellers between the Algarve and Andalusia. There are train and bus terminuses and a ferry boat connection with Ayamonte on the Spanish side of the river. The ferry used to be the only way in and out of the Algarve at Vila Real, but an elegant bridge a couple of kilometers upriver now carries most of the two-way traffic.

INLAND ALGARVE

The Barrocal, a band of gently undulating hills and fertile valleys sitting on a limestone base, runs parallel to the south coast, wedged between the coastal plain and the serras. Running most of the Algarve's length, it is virtually one elongated orchard brimming with almonds and olives, oranges and lemons, peaches and apricots, figs and pomegranates. The largest inland towns and villages, and many scattered smallholdings, are located along this band.

The two main ranges of hills higher up, Serra de Monchique and Serra de Caldeirão, are much more sparsely populated. They are clothed in low scrub, mainly holm oak and flowering cistus bushes, or densely forested with cork oak, pine and eucalyptus.

PROMISED LAND

"We crossed several beautiful mountain streams. It is a strange country – exactly the Holy Land views, mountain all around swelling, breasting, surging like a sea.

"After six long, long, very long leagues we reached the lowlands of Algarve. From the last height the coast opened and we saw Vila Real, Ayamonte and Castro Marim. We had escaped the wilderness and this was our Land of Promise."

Robert Southey, English Poet Laureate, on his visit to the Algarve in April 1801.

Alferce

At an elevation of 454 metres, **MONCHIQUE** is the Algarve's highest town. It is also the most northerly, situated about 25km north of Portimão and approached from that direction on the EN266, a particularly lovely drive in late February and early March, when brilliant yellow mimosa bushes are in bloom along the roadside.

On the way up to Monchique, stop at the little village of **CALDAS DE MONCHIQUE**. It has been a spa for at least 2000 years. It sits in a well-wooded ravine which resounds in early summer to the song of nightingales.

The Romans appreciated the curative powers of the waters here in the days of Augustus Caesar. In medieval times, King João II sought a cure for dropsy. In recent years, many visitors suffering from rheumatism, back pains, respiratory and muscular complaints have benefited from water therapy treatments in the Hotel Termal, one of four small hotels at Caldas.

At the top end of the village there is a tree-shaded walk and a picnic area, a square with cafés and a nearby pavilion where you can sample natural spring water as it gushes straight out of the ground.

Caldas de Monchique

The restaurants on the right-hand side of the main road between Caldas de Monchique and beyond the town of Monchique are renowned for chicken piri-piri lunches.

Shops in the town of Monchique, 6km further up the road from Caldas, sells products grown or handmade in the surrounding hills. Light furniture including 'scissors' chairs, leather goods, basketwork, woollen sweaters, smoked ham and honey are among the specialities.

Take a stroll around the narrow, cobbled streets near the parish church, with its Manueline doorway and poly-

Arbutus berries

chromatic tiles. Eating in a restaurant or café around here is optional, but drinking is obligatory. Find a hole-in-the-wall bar and ask for a shot of *medronho*, a clear spirit made from arbutus berries. Make sure you ask for *caseiro* medronho, meaning homemade. You might like it and come away with a litre of medronho moonshine concealed in a soft drink bottle. The ladies will probably prefer the taste of *brandymel*, a honey-flavoured brandy liqueur.

From the main square in Monchique, follow the road signs for **FÓIA,** the Algarve's highest point at just over 900 metres. The road climbs up beyond the tree-line to the rocky summit. On clear days, there are fine views and tracks to be explored, despite the forest of telecommunications towers and aerials and a no-go military compound.

There is no alternative route back to Monchique, but a scenic option to return to the coast is to veer left, just as you are leaving Monchique, at the road sign to Alferce. On arrival at Alferce, don't bother turning into the village. Follow the signs pointing right to Fornalha and Monchicão. A good tarred road then takes

Near Fóia

Silves

you all the way down the Odelouca valley to emerge near the village of Porto de Lagos, either on the Monchique-Portimão or Portimão-Silves roads.

SILVES is at the heart of one of Portugal's most prolific citrus growing areas. It also used to be a substantial cork processing centre but there is little evidence of that today, except in a museum in the Fábrica do Inglês, a once thriving cork factory, now a restaurant complex.

The two most visible buildings in Silves, and the ones every visitor comes to see, are a red sandstone castle that would not look out of place on a chocolate box, and a red and white cathedral next to it. They are reminders that, in medieval times, this was the scene of horrific battles between Christians and Muslims.

The Romans had a secure settlement at Silves, but it was the Moors who built it into a fine, prosperous town with gleaming minarets and bazaars. They called it Xelb and made it their regional capital. It was a place of peace and plenty in the 12th century until Portuguese forces, aided by thousands of English, German and Flemish Crusaders on their way to the Holy Land, attacked the town in 1189.

Crusader memorial

They razed everything outside the town walls and lay siege to the castle.

The siege lasted six weeks and ended with an agreement by the Muslims to surrender, if the Christians allowed them

Silves Cathedral

to leave for the Moorish city of Seville in Spain, taking with them whatever possessions they could carry. Portugal's King Sancho I agreed. To his horror, the Crusaders mercenaries stripped the defeated and departing Moors of everything of value, and then went on a looting spree through what was left of the town. After three days of this, the King was so appalled that he ordered the Crusaders back to their ships at anchor in the river below.

The following year, England's Richard the Lionheart helped defend Silves from a counter-attack by the Muslims. The year after that, yet another attack and a month-long siege by the Muslims exacted revenge for the 1189 humiliation. It was 1231 before the castle finally capitulated to the Christian forces of Afonso III. His statue stands, sword in hand, just inside the castle gates today.

Amid the jacaranda trees, oleander shrubs and flowerbeds, the Moorish cistern that once held sufficient water for defenders to survive a year-long siege is now permanently closed. Apart from sections of the walls, the only Moorish feature left in the castle is a well 65-metres deep.

Another Moorish well is the central feature of a small, modern and nicely arranged museum in a side street not far from the castle.

The reconquest of Silves was celebrated with the building of a cathedral on the site of a mosque. Much restored and rebuilt over the years, it contains the tombs of some of the Crusaders who died here in battle.

The Crusaders arrived at Silves on ships which in those days were able to sail all the way up the river. Silting and dam building have reduced the river to a tidal stream. The oldest of the two bridges which straddle it, the Ponte Romana, is old but it is probably not as old as its name suggests. Doubt also surrounds the origin and age of an intricately carved piece of sculpture, known as the Cross of Portugal, situated on the left-hand side of the main road leaving Silves for São Bartolomeu de Messines.

MESSINES, as the name is usually abbreviated to, is not really on the tourist map and, for that reason, it is a good place to visit for those interested in getting a feel for the 'real' Algarve. As with all Algarve towns, the parish church is the most obvious building, in this case a nicely

proportioned baroque structure dating from at least the last quarter of the 16th century. You can't miss it on the main east-west road through the centre of town.

In common with several other Algarve towns and villages, the people of Messines pay homage to the memory of a local man of letters, in this case João de Deus (1830-1896) His most acclaimed work was a collection of poems entitled *A Field of Flowers*. His former home next to the church is now a museum and library. In springtime, fields of flowers still abound in the countryside around this peaceful town.

Salir

In **ALTE**, 11km to the east of Messines on the EN124, local literary fame rests with the poet Candido Guerreiro (1871-1953). Some of his verse, all in Portuguese of course, has been reproduced on tile panels which adorn the leafy *fontes* (springs) for which Alte is best known.

Barbecuing chouriço

Both **PADERNE** to the south and **SALIR** to the east of Alte are very old settlements. They still have vestiges of their Moorish past. Each has castle ruins - and that's about as lively as it gets around here, except for annual community get-togethers (*bailes*) to celebrate the local patron saints.

One of the biggest red letter days each year in the hilltop village of **QUERENÇA** is a smoked sausage festival in January. Called *chouriço* in Portuguese, the sausages are locally made and considered a great delicacy. The church square in Querença is an ideal place to pause and have lunch, with or without *chouriço*, during a drive around the Barrocal. To work up an appetite, or walk off the lunch, take a stroll along the river in a nearby protected beauty spot called Fonte da Benémola.

Querença is situated between the EN124 Alte-Salir road and, 10km to the south, the Algarve's largest inland town, **LOULÉ**. There are remnants of old castle walls in the centre of Loulé, but the town is more associated with light-heartedness than history. It really comes alive during the annual carnival festivities (before Lent, usually February). The merrymaking doesn't quite rival that in Rio de Janeiro, but people from all over the Algarve converge on the town for a long weekend of floats and fancy-dress parades, high spirits, high jinks and sometimes practical jokes involving fireworks, flour or paint. If you intend to attend carnival events, wear old clothes.

Loulé market

A much more sober pageant is held annually on Easter Sunday. A heavy and elaborate image of the Virgin Mary, a version known as Mãe Soberana (the Sovereign Mother), is carried in procession from the hilltop Chapel of Nossa Senhora da Piedade, about 1km outside the town. The return procession, a much bigger and more festive occasion, takes place two weeks later.

There is a lively atmosphere in Loulé every Saturday morning at the food market in Largo de Gago Coutino and the gypsy market in streets off Largo de São Francisco. Halfway between these two squares stand the castle walls with a museum and a tourist information office inside. In the streets round about you will come across dimly-lit workshops with craftsmen beating copper, stitching leather or selling wrought-iron, cane furniture, basketwork and embroidered goods.

On the south-facing, almond-covered slopes, 13km east of Loulé, lies the much quieter town of **SÃO BRÁS DE ALPORTEL**. It is overlooked by one of the Algarve's two pousada hotels (the other being at Sagres), but it is far from being a hub of tourism. Essentially a small market town, São Brás largely lives in the past.

It still takes pride in the fact that this was the birthplace, in the 12th century, of a Moorish poet, Ibne Ammar. Faro bishops used to escape the midsummer heat of the coast and take refuge in the relative cool-

Cork bark

ness of a foothill hermitage. Cork is still produced but not on the international scale of yesteryear. One of São Brás' main attraction to visitors is an ethnographic museum, specializing in traditional Algarve costumes, carriages and farm implements.

A few kilometers south of São Brás, the big attractions of **ESTÓI** are its curious 18th-century country mansion and nearby Roman ruins. The mansion is known locally as a *palácio*. Only the gardens may be visited. The Roman ruins down the road at Milreu are of a nobleman's house with the remnants, on the roadside, of a nymphaerium, a temple dedicated to water.

BARRANCO DO VELHO, 12km east of Salir, 13km north

Estói palácio gardens

Cova dos Mouros exhibit

of São Brás, just under 20km from Loulé, is the gateway to the remote, wholly undeveloped northeast section of the Algarve. Having driven up through the rolling hills, you

arrive on a plateau, a wonderful wilderness expanse with little habitation except in **CACHOPO** and **MARTIM LONGO**.

Of special interest in this area is the Parque Mineiro Cova dos Mouros, a Moorish mine park. Located between Martim Longo and Vaqueiros on the EN 506, the well-signposted park offers a short walk through a long period of time, about 5,000 years give or take a few centuries.

Past Martim Longo, the long lonely EN124 road heads eastward until it crosses the north-south EN122 up from Vila Real. It then heads 6km further on, finally arriving in **ALCOUTIM** on the banks of the Guadiana. With its medieval fortress ruins, Alcoutim, a delightful backwater village, looks across the river to similar ruins above the neat little Spanish town of San Lucar.

ALENTEJO

The Alentejo is Portugal's poorest and most sparsely populated province. Its gently undulating plains are vast vistas of corn and cork oak trees, with seasonal splashes of vivid yellow rape and sunflowers under cultivation. This is the most agricultural of Portugal's provinces, with little reliance on tourism.

As in the west of the Algarve, wildly beautiful beaches punctuate the coastline of the Alentejo, but as in the Algarve, there is no coast road as such. The westerly route to Lisbon runs up from Odeceixe through Odemira and Alcácer do Sal.

The fastest and most central route is on the Lisbon-bound A2 which takes off from the A22 north of Albufeira and zaps up past Ourique and Grândola. The Alentejo's most interesting towns, however, are over in the east towards the Spanish border.

Mértola, Beja, Évora and Estremoz and any number of fascinating villages are easily reached from lateral roads off the A2 or on the EN122 which runs directly north from Vila Real de Stº António.

Mértola

LISBON

A city of ancient origin, modern Lisbon is one of Europe's most agreeable capitals, an attractive metropolis of manageable proportion which is easy to explore. The centre of the city is a hubbub of vigorous business activity and frantic traffic, but there is an old-fashioned elegance in its broad avenues, cobbled streets, clanking trams and faded 18th and 19th century facades.

From the Algarve, the capital can be easily reached by car, coach or train. On arrival you cross the river Tagus either on the San Francisco-style April 25 bridge or on the newer and longer Vasco da Gama bridge. There is plenty of hotel and guesthouse accommodation, but check on availability beforehand.

The April 25 bridge leads to the historic, administrative, business and shopping centre of the city: Praça do Comércio, the squares of Rossio and Restauradores, Avenida da Liberdade, Belém. There is a panoramic view of downtown Lisbon from the Castelo de São Jorge.

Left:Discoveries Monument

Below: Praça do Comércio

Mosteiro dos Jerónimos

The most impressive building in Lisbon is the Mosteiro dos Jerónimos, founded in 1499 to commemorate Vasco da Gama's discovery of the sea route to India. The largest of many fine museums and galleries is the Fundação Calouste Gulbenkian.

The bars and restaurants of the Bairro Alto district are where it all happens after dark.

The Vasco da Gama bridge is the quickest route to the Parque das Nações (former Expo site) on the east side of Lisbon. This is where major concerts and exhibitions are held. There is good hotel accommodation, and easy access to the city centre by the metro.

Below: Modern Comercial Centre in Parque das Nações
Left: Typical street of Lisbon (Elevador da Bica)

SHORT VISITS TO SPAIN

The A22 motorway, the Guadiana bridge and the absence of immigration or customs formalities make a visit to Spain by car almost effortless. One precaution, though, before setting out: make sure you have insurance cover for Spain as well as Portugal.

The best places for a Spanish trip:

- Ayamonte
- La Rabida and Palos
- Cota Doñana National Park
- Seville

Turn first right at the end of the bridge and follow the signs to the centre of **AYAMONTE** for an instant change of cultural. It may be a border town, but Ayamonte, on the east bank of the river opposite Vila Real, is very obviously a part of Spain, not Portugal. Pause in the square by the little harbour in the heart of town or drive around to the resort of Isla Canelas, or the fishing port of Ilha Cristina, for a glass or two of *fino* (sherry) and a plate of *tapas*.

About an hour's drive from Ayamonte, past the port city of Huelva, **LA RABIDA** is the monastery where Columbus spent a considerable amount of time planning and praying before setting out on his first voyage to the New World in 1492. His actual point of departure was the nearby port of **PALOS DE LA FRONTEIRA**. The well where the *Santa Maria*, the *Niña* and *Pinta* took on supplies of fresh water for the voyage is still preserved and there are replicas of the three boats open to visitors. La Rabida and Palos de la Fronteira are situated south of Huelva, on the other side of the Rio Tinto.

From Palos, a long, straight road runs parallel to the coast past Mazagón down to the modern resort of Matalascañas. It is only a short drive from there to the **COTO DOÑANA** national park main entrance at Acebuche. As one the greatest wildlife reserves of southern Europe, Doñana is carefully protected. The only way to see it is on a morning or afternoon official tour starting from the Acebuche reception centre. Ring in advance to book seats.

For those wishing to stay overnight, there is a comfort-able parador at Mazagón, and more modestly priced hotel rooms in Matalascañas and El Rocío. The latter, one of Spain's best-known places of pilgrimage, is a fascinating place to visit in itself.

SEVILLE, the capital of Andalusia, is one of the most elegant and exciting cities in the whole of Spain. It can be reached by car in an hour or so from the Guadiana bridge. Parking can be a problem, though, so consider taking a bus excursion from the Algarve. It's a fun city after dark so, if possible, stay over-night. There are masses of cheap to expensive hotel rooms, but book in advance.

Top places to see in Seville by day: the Cathedral with its Giralda tower; the Alcázar palace; Parque Maria Luisa with its Plaza de España; the Belas Arts Museum, second only in Spain to the Prado in Madrid.

At night much of the action is in the tapas bars and fla-menco restaurants in the pic-turesque back streets and small squares of the Santa Cruz and El Arenal districts, all within walking distance or a short taxi ride of the Cathedral.

*Page100: Ayamonte square
Page 101: Columbus statue
This page left: Sevillanas.
Right: Seville Cathedral.*

THINGS TO DO

WINING

Portugal has long been an important wine producing country, most famous, of course, for its port and Madeira dessert wines. It has also had phenomenal export success with rosé wines, particularly 'Mateus Rosé' and 'Lancers'. In recent years, its reputation for good and rela-

tively inexpensive red and white table wines has soared internationally. Great things are predicted for the future of the Portuguese wine industry. And, at long last, the Algarve region is for the first time producing wine of quality.

Vinho verde, green wine peculiar to Portugal, is so called because it is young, not because of its colour. Produced in the northwest of the country, it is a light, slightly bubbly, lunchtime drink, particularly refreshing with fish, chicken or salads on hot summer days.

You are more or less assured of a decent glass of *tinto* or *branco* table wine if it comes from a bottle with a Dão, Douro or Bairrada label on it. They are three of the country's foremost demarcated regions. Red and white wines from the Alentejo are good value and are getting better all the time. Look for labels showing the place of origin as Borba, Vidigueira or Reguengos.

Algarve wines had never been highly rated until Sir Cliff Richard, with the best available advice from experts of renown, began producing 'Vida Nova' red from grapes grown in his vineyard near Guia. Just two years after the 'Vida Nova' debut of 2001, the project was expanded with the setting up of a boutique winery at Quinta do Miradouro to produce all future Vida Nova and other local vintages. Visitors are welcome to tour the winery, located behind the Algarve Shopping complex in Guia.

In restaurants you have the choice of ordering from the wine list (*lista de vinhos*) or settling for the house wine (*vinho da casa*). As a rule of thumb, the better the restaurant, the better the house wine.

The least known of the **port** family is dry white port, an excellent aperitif akin to sherry. It should be served chilled.

The other port wines enjoy a worldwide reputation for excellence as after-dinner drinks. They come from grapes grown exclusively in the Douro valley in the north of Portugal. All are produced in wineries in Vila Nova de Guia, across

the river from the northern city of Oporto. Ruby and tawny ports are not expensive. Prices can rise dramatically, though, for a special year 'vintage' or 'late bottled' port.

Portugal also produces cheap **brandies**, such as 'Macieira' and 'Constantino', *medronho* spirit and several potent and colourless firewaters (*figo* and *bagaço*). The most popular local **liqueurs** are *brandymel*, a combination of medronho and honey, *ginginha*, which is made from cherries, and almond-based *amêndoa amarga*.

The most noteworthy point about **spirits** such as whisky, gin, vodka, whisky and so on, is that optic measures are not often used. The hand-poured Portuguese measures are generous, well over the top compared with the UK.

Imported British and German **beers** are widely available in bottles, cans or barrels, but Portuguese-made lager is by far the biggest seller.

DINING

This is one of the great delights of the Algarve and dining out is still relatively cheap. The range of restaurants is enormous. The number seemed to reach saturation point years ago, but new places continue to open all the time. The competition keeps standards up and prices down.

Broadly speaking, the type of food on offer is either international or typically Portuguese. The hotels and top restaurants concentrate on **international cuisine**, though they may have one or two Portuguese dishes on their menus. The great majority of more modest restaurants serve dishes that are typical of Portugal as a whole or the Algarve region in particular.

Portuguese dishes are usually prepared from fresh fish or meat and in-season veg-

etables. It has to be said, however, that there is a depressing sameness about many of the Portuguese menus.

Foreigners have come to the Algarve and set up restaurants specialising in **national dishes** characteristic of their homeland. Thus you can find French, Belgian, German, Austrian, Scandinavian, Chinese, Indian, Indonesian and Vietnamese-style cooking as well as roast beef and Yorkshire pud.

Fast food has gained a foothold in the Algarve, but it is not in any way a serious threat to the vast majority of restaurants, including the most modest ones, which continue to serve proper, healthy meals.

Vegetarians have not been well catered for in the Algarve in the past, but that is slowly changing. Although all locally grown vegetables are strictly seasonal - a glut one month, unobtainable the next - there is usually plenty of fresh produce for those who shun meat. In recognition of a significant demand, a growing number of restaurants are now including a few imaginative vegetarian dishes on their menus, but the choice for vegetarians dining out is often tediously restricted to salads or omelettes.

Confronted by a bewildering array of **restaurants**, visitors can quickly sort out what's what without much difficulty. To gauge popularity and atmosphere, have a peek through the door. The busier, the better is not a bad rule of thumb. Menus are often on display outside, in English as well as Portuguese, so you can see what's available and check on prices.

No sooner have you sat down than the waiter will arrive with the **couvert**. This may be just a basket of bread and sachets of butter or it may run to little plates of olives, fresh goat's cheese and tins of paté. Don't get the idea that this is free. If you eat it, it will appear on your bill. If you don't want it, send it back and you won't be charged.

The choice of **starters** (*entradas*) in a Portuguese restaurant is usually limited to shellfish or soup. Cockles (*berbigão*) are the least expensive of the shellfish. Check on the price (often quoted per kilo) before you go ordering piles of prawns (*gambas*).

Soups, whether seafood (*sopa de peixe*), vegetable (*sopa de legumes*) or a special cabbage broth (*caldo verde*), are nearly always homemade. No doubt *sopa à Alentejana* is good for you

but be warned, it is a watery mix of bread, garlic and coriander with an egg floating around on top.

Facing the Atlantic, the Portuguese have always been a race of seafarers and so it is not surprising that the Algarve is well known for its fresh **seafoods**: whole lobster and crawfish, dressed crabs, all sorts of prawns, tuna and swordfish steaks, big sea bream and sea bass, succulent sole…the list goes on and on. Sadly, apart from sardines, none of it is cheap any more.

Freshness is all important. Fish must have come out of the sea that same day. You should be able to tell: fish is often on display behind glass in a cooler or brought to the table on a platter for examination before ordering. Look for clear eyes and shiny flesh.

Cataplana is an Algarve seafood speciality. It can be made with various ingredients, but the most usual are clams or mussels, with strips of bacon or pieces of pork, pressure cooked with spiced sausage (*chouriço*), garlic, onions and olive oil. Cataplana takes its name from the tightly closing, clam-shaped, copper pan used for the cooking.

Bacalhau, absolutely beloved by the Portuguese, is nothing more than dried, salted cod. It may sound boring, but it is said the Portuguese have a different bacalhau recipe for every day of the year. The one foreigners are most likely to enjoy is Bacalhau à Brás, which comes with potatoes, eggs, onion and garlic.

Arroz de marisco, mixed seafood served with rice, is usually well liked by visitors too, but stuffed squid (*lulas recheadas*) has a more limited appeal.

For those who can't be bothered with the bones, swordfish (*peixe espardarte*) can be a real treat. Tuna (*atum*) is a dark-fleshed fish, also served as cutlets, usually with fried onions. Fresh tuna is usually only available in spring and early summer. Frozen tuna is available all year round, but freezing dries it and destroys the taste.

Sea Bass (*robalo*) comes as a steak or cooked whole. Its firm white flesh is prized by the best hotel restaurants. It is also often available, caught by local anglers, at simple beach bars.

Sardines (*sardinhas*) have always been an Algarve staple. They are at their plumpest and tastiest in summer. Charcoal-grilled is the only way to have them cooked. To eat them, don't fiddle about with a knife and fork. Do it the Algarve way and use your fingers. Here's how: place a sardine on a piece of bread. Pick up the bread and nibble at the flesh from the tail to the gills. Take care not to eat the innards; they taste bitter. Turn the fish over and repeat.

Charcoal-grilled chicken

(*frango no churrasco*) is another Algarve favourite and many people like it cooked with hot piri-piri sauce. In other countries, chicken is often boring and bland. In the Algarve it is always really tasty, though invariably served with nothing more than chips. It has become a Sunday lunch tradition in the Algarve to take the family for a chicken piri-piri lunch to one of the restaurants in Guia or on the road up to Monchique.

Pork is the meat most relished by the Algarvios and it is the most consistently good. It comes as chops (*costeletas de porco*), as a fillet (*lombo*), sliced (*febras*) or spare ribs (*entrecosto*). Unless you fancy pigs' ears and other unspeakable parts of the anatomy, avoid the locally popular concoction called *Cozido á Portuguesa*.

Lamb is served as chops or in a Portuguese stew called *Caldeirada de Cabrito,* which includes potatoes, peppers, tomatoes, onions and garlic, and is often spiced up with piri-piri sauce. You can always ask for more piri-piri if it is not spiced up enough.

Beef in Portuguese restaurants may not be quite what you expect. Beef is not hung prior to cooking here, nor is it prepared as elsewhere. Thus, it often arrives at the table tough and disappointing to the taste buds. Steaks are best ordered only in restaurants with a reputation for good fillets.

For **desserts**, the choice does not usually run beyond mousse chocolate, crème caramel (*pudim flan*), rice pudding (*arroz doce*), almond tart (*tarte de amêndoa*), cream cake (*tarte de natas*) or Olá ice cream.

Of the modest selection of **cheeses** produced in Portugal, the best are *Queijo da Serra* from the country's highest mountain range, and cheddar-like *Queijo da Ilha* from the Azores.

MUSIC

Some restaurants regularly feature live **fado** music, Portugal's equivalent to Spain's flamenco. From its sleazy African origins, fado has come a long way and now occupies a place of high respectability. To guitar accompaniment, fado is sung with great passion and often elicits rapturous applause.

There are two resident traditional **jazz** bands, both made up of highly experienced expat musicians. There are also a number of talented British and Portuguese exponents of modern jazz. The best groups and individuals can be heard in specialist clubs, restaurants and festivals.

Portugal's historic ties with colonies abroad means there is a special appreciation here for **African** and **Brazilian** styles of music. **Rock** is ever popular and big name pop groups occasionally perform in one of the football stadiums or hotels. The superstar shows, however, are nearly all in Lisbon.

Surprisingly, perhaps, in a holiday destination like the Algarve, the most widely performed music is **classica**l. The region has its own orchestra - Orquestra do Algarve – which gives frequent performances. The Algarve International Music Festival is easily the best funded and most exten-

sive of the many annual festivals. It is held from April to June, at venues all along the coast, with performances by prominent international and Portuguese orchestras, chamber ensembles, soloists and ballet groups. Throughout the year, local or Lisbon-based musicians give recitals at cultural centres in Lagos, Lagoa, Almancil and Faro.

FINE ARTS

New exhibitions of **painting** and **sculpture** by resident or visiting artists frequently open in the Algarve's many art galleries. Old paintings and carvings are on permanent display in various museums and churches. Increasingly, the Algarve is being recognised as an ideal place for painting holidays. Student courses are offered.

Hand-painted tiles, *azulejos*, are the region's most distinctive traditional art form. The oldest and best panels of geometrically patterned tiles and Biblical scenes are to be found in churches.

ENTERTAINMENT

There are three modest **casinos**, the best at Vilamoura, with two smaller ones at

Monte Gordo and Praia da Rocha. The Vilamoura casino features a nightly cabaret show. Glamorous shows in the Algarve are rare, however, and the better hotels make do with rather tamer programmes of traditional folk music and dancing. Some hotels have dance-floors with small combos playing relatively modern music. The more youthful alternative are **discos**, of which there are several along the coast, all well advertised.

There are lots of **festivals** and *feiras* throughout the year. Almost anything is justification enough for special evenings of eating, drinking, music and dancing in the streets. A few of the bigger festivals focus on sausages (Querença in January), beer (Silves in July), shellfish (Olhão in August), handicrafts (Loulé in July) and folk music (all over the place but culminating in Praia da Rocha in September).

SHOPPING

If you are on a self-catering holiday or you just want to pick up a few goodies for a picnic or barbecue, the most entertaining places to buy all types of fresh fish, meat, vegetables and fruit are the **municipal markets**. Everything is colourfully laid out on stalls under one roof, or in the case of the biggest municipal markets, two roofs.

Most markets open mornings only, Monday to Saturday. Albufeira and Faro markets are open every morning, Sunday included. Prices are usually scrawled on blackboards or pieces of cardboard and they almost always refer to the price per kilo. The only vegetables and fruit on sale are those in season locally.

To shop economically at supermarkets, mini-markets or any other sort of grocery store, the key is to avoid imported brands. The Portuguese-produced equivalent of corn flakes, baked beans or whatever is probably of equal quality and almost certainly cheaper.

Monday is not a good day to shop for fish as Algarve fishermen generally have Sunday night off.

If you find the meats in butchers' cold counters presented or cut in an unfamiliar manner, don't worry. The butcher will cut to order anyway you like.

'Gypsy markets' are something else again. They move from town to town on a fixed daily and weekly schedule. They are always cluttered and congested, full of animation

MONTHLY MARKET SCHEDULE

The following is the schedule for regional or gypsy markets at the time of going to press. To be sure there have been no changes since, check with any tourist information office.

Albufeira	*First and third Tuesday*
Lagoa	*Second Sunday (except July & August)*
Lagos	*First Saturday*
Loulé	*Every Saturday*
Monchique	*Second Friday*
Portimão	*First Monday (except August)*
São Brás	*Every Saturday*
Quarteira	*Every Wednesday*
Silves	*Third Monday*
Tavira	*Third Saturday*
Vila do Bispo	*First Thursday*

and sometimes, genuine bargains. You can buy anything from light bulbs to livestock, but as a visitor you will probably be more interested in remarkably low-priced footwear and clothes, items manufactured in Portugal in a big way for export.

The **handicraft** or *artesanato* shops at intervals along main roads are choc-a-bloc with baskets, mats, table cloths, woollen sweaters, cork things and, more than anything else, cheap pottery. Browsers are welcome. Take your time in finding souvenirs or gifts to take home.

Higher quality Portuguese crafted products are to be found in shops specialising in porcelain, pewter, full-lead crystal and filigree gold and silver.

Normal **shop hours** are 9am to 1pm, 3pm to 7pm. Closed Saturday afternoons and all day Sunday.

SPORTS

Golf is the most popular participation sport in the Algarve. It can be played all-year-round and most of the Algarve's courses, which include several of the finest in continental Europe, are open to players regardless of their handicap.

It is a surprisingly well-established sport in Portugal. The first course was built near Oporto in 1890. The first

course in the Algarve was being played in 1920s, but it was very rough and ready. The father of the modern game in the Algarve was Henry Cotton. He designed the Penina course in the mid 1960s and went on to design two others, Vale do Lobo and Alto Golf.

Certain green fee discounts and an economical 'passport' scheme are on offer. During the summer, cut-price green fees are available for midday and evening tee off times.

Information, including playing tips, on all of the Algarve's courses, is contained in a monthly magazine, *Algarve Golf Guide*, available free at clubhouse reception desks.

The most authoritative and

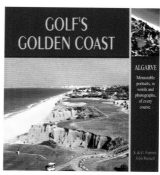

comprehensive book on the subject is *Golf's Golden Coast* by S & G Farmer and John Russell.

There are many **riding centres** with Lusitano, or part Lusitano, horses for adults and ponies for children. Those who have not been in a saddle for a while may want to take a few lessons before riding out over sand dunes or on trails through pine forests. Lessons are also available for beginners and for disabled riders.

Tennis is another all-year-round sport with courts available at hourly rates. Apart from the courts attached to specific hotels and smaller complexes, some of which offer coaching, there are two major tennis centres, at Vale do Lobo near Almancil and Clube Carvoeiro west of Carvoeiro village.

Lagos aerodrome has a well-established **micro-lighting** centre. Trial flights are available for anyone thinking of taking up the sport. Beginners can sign up for courses leading to a solo licence. Courses are typically 10 to 15 hours of instruction stretched over two or three weeks. Contact: 282 762906

There are several **fitness and leisure clubs** with multisports, health and beauty facilities. The best are Barringtons at Vale do Lobo, Browns of Vilamoura, the Sports Centre at Burgau and Parque da Floresta near Budens, west of Lagos.

There are locations and conditions to suit all water sports. The combination of force five afternoon winds and calm seas is perfect for **windsurfing**. Boards can be hired at many beaches.

The sheltered, sandy-bottomed lagoons of the eastern Algarve and the Arade reservoir between Silves and Messines are the best places for **water-skiing**.

Scuba divers prefer the central and western south coast where most of the rocky reefs and wrecks are concentrated. There are several diving centres with fully qualified instructors.

Praia da Marinha, between Armação de Pera and Carvoeiro, is just one of many good beaches for **snorkelling** along the south and west coasts. Water temperatures are such that a wetsuit is needed outside of July and August.

Praia da Rocha is popular for **surfing,** but serious surfers find the best Atlantic roll-

ers on the southwest and west coasts, at beaches such Zavial and Amado.

The prevailing north-westerly winds in summer are perfect for **sailing**. Lagos Bay is a favourite for dinghy sailors. The Algarve's three established yacht marinas are at Lagos, Portimão and Vilamoura. The newest marina is at Albufeira.

BOAT TRIPS

Game-fishing boats are based in Vilamoura and Portimão. Blue and mako sharks are the normal quarry. Boats trolling in Algarve waters sometime catch very much rarer blue or black marlin.

Coarse fishing boats stay closer to the coast. They stop six or eight miles out at rocky seabed sites with bottom feeders such as bass and bream. As on game boats, rods and tackle are laid on for visitors.

Coastal sightseeing boat trips operate throughout the year, weather permitting. The two most scenic sections of the south coast are between Armação de Pêra and the mouth of the river Arade at Ferragudo, and from Lagos round the Ponte de Piedade headland. Day trips (10.0am-6.0pm) and half-day trips (10.0am-2.0pm or 2.0pm-6.0pm) depart from Portimão and Lagos. Shorter trips operate from these two harbours and a number of beaches.

River cruises from Vila Real de Stº António sail 20km up the Guadiana as far as Foz de Odeleite, where there is a pause for lunch. The shorter river cruises from the quayside at Portimão go up on the high tide as far as Silves.

HISTORICAL SIGHTS

Visitors interested in archaeology or history will need a car to get around properly. One of the places they should visit is the Neolithic dolmen site at Alcalar, 5kms inland and signposted on the EN125 between the roundabout turn-off to Alvor and the entrance to the Penina hotel. There are megaliths or menhirs scattered all over the Algarve hinterland. Those in the east are difficult to find. The easiest to find are just south of Vila do Bispo in the west.

Roman ruins dating from the earliest centuries of the first millennium can be visited at Milreu (near Estói), Vilamoura (near the marina) and Abicada (7kms west of Portimão). The main medieval fortresses are at Sagres, Silves

and Castro Marim, with remnants of Moorish fortifications at Aljezur and Paderne. Museums at Faro, Lagos, Silves and Moncarapacho contain relics from the Neolithic through Roman, Visigoth, Moorish and medieval Christian periods.

BIRDWATCHING

Naturalists will find that the Algarve is extraordinarily rich in fauna and flora. Diligence and patience are often needed to find the most interesting or unusual species. Among the best places for both birds and plants are Cape St. Vincent, the Serra de Monchique, Odelouca Valley, Alvor estuary, Salgados marshes, the Ria Formosa and Castro Marim nature reserves and the plains of the southeastern Alentejo.

The marshes of the Ria Formosa, including those on a trail within Quinta do Lago, are an important refuge in Europe for the rare purple gallinule. Cattle and little egrets, white storks, black-winged stilts, greater flamingos, collared pratincoles, alpine swifts, woodchat shrikes, bee-eaters and azure-winged magpies are just a few of the many species which may be unfamiliar to birdwatchers from northern Europe. All are here in summer.

The spring and autumn migration periods bring many other unusual species. Cape St. Vincent in September and October is especially interesting. Birdwatchers gather there for seabird and raptor watches.

Resident ornithologist Simon Wates (282 798044) leads small groups on outings in southern Portugal and Spain.

NATURE RAMBLES

The almond blossom of January is followed by glorious displays of mimosa in February. In March and April, cistus bushes are blooming over huge areas of the uncultivated countryside. From March to June several varieties of orchid are prolific, none more so than the bee orchids.

Judas trees and jacaranda trees are looking their best in May when there is also an abundance of wildflowers, including yellow and red vetchlings, pimpernels, periwinkles, French lavender, crown daisies and Bermuda buttercups.

With such a profusion of wildflowers, it follows that there are a great many butterflies, including Europe's biggest and brightest: the monarch, tiger, swallowtail and false swallowtail.

The Mediterranean chameleon and ocellated lizard are but two of a variety of reptiles and amphibians. The most frequently seen lizards, usually hunting for insects on the walls of houses, are harmless geckoes.

Otters frequent all of the Algarve's freshwater rivers and will venture into the sea in search of fish if their freshwater habitat dries up in summer. Of the other mammals, the most often encountered are the Egyptian mongoose and the genet. The remotest hill areas are thought to harbour small numbers of the world's rarest cat, the Iberian Lynx.

Visitors are welcome to join nature walks organised by the Liga para a Protecção da Natureza (League for the Protection of Nature) on the first Saturday of each month, except August (inquiries 282 789359).

DRIVES

To really enjoy a day out in the countryside, start fairly early, don't rush and take time to linger a while at the places of particular interest. Fill up with petrol before you go because petrol stations are scarce in some areas inland.

On the other hand, refreshments along the way are never difficult to find.

Drive A takes in the most interesting places associated with the Age of Discovery, starting with Lagos. It includes scenic countryside, wooded hills and a spectacular section of coastline.

Having walked around Lagos, particularly the stretch between the Praça Gil Eanes and the little fort at the harbour mouth, drive westward on the EN125 past the villages of Espiche, Budens and Raposeira to Vila do Bispo, where you bear left toward Sagres.

At the first roundabout in Sagres, straight ahead leads to the cark park outside the imposing *fortaleza*. A visit to the fortress (small entrance charge) is not mandatory, but a close-up view of the lighthouse at Cape St Vincent is.

After the lighthouse, drive all the way back to Vila do Bispo and then take the EN268 northward towards Aljezur. At the village of Carrapateira, turn left off the main road at signs for 'praia' and 'Sítio do Rio'. Follow this rough road anti-clockwise all the way around until you are back on the main road, having sampled some of the most dramatic coastal scenery in the Algarve.

Continue northward, past the village of Bordeira and on to Aljezur. Drive up to the fort at the top of the hill for panoramic views before crossing the bridge linking the old and new halves of town. At the roundabout, take the Lisbon road, turning left shortly thereafter at a signpost indicating 'praia'. You end up at the Paraíso do Mar restaurant overlooking Praia da Amoreira, a good place for a cool drink or a full lunch.

On returning to the Aljezur roundabout, take the Monchique road. Up you go into wooded hills, eventually passing terraced fields beyond Marmalete and Casais. This road ultimately ends at a T-junction by the quarry at Nave. Turn right towards Portimão. Soon you can turn right again off the main road and refresh yourself at

Caldas de Monchique.

After that, it's all downhill towards the EN125 and A22.

Drive B gives an insight into Algarve rural life by meandering through cork and almond-covered foothills and along valleys filled with orange groves. There are remnants of the region's Roman and Moorish heritage in several villages and small towns, beginning with Estói.

Access to Estói is easy from either direction on the A2 motorway. Before the village, a signpost indicates the 'Ruinas Romanas' of Milreu (entrance charge, open 9.30am-12.30pm, 2.0pm-5pm, closed Mondays and public holidays).

After looking at the ruins, carry on into the village proper and find the Estói Palácio (free, 9.30am-12.30pm, 2.0pm-5.30pm, closed Sundays and public holidays). It is tucked away to the left of the parish church. Unfortunately, the *palácio* is permanently closed and only the gardens may be viewed.

It is only 7km from Estói to our next stop, São Brás de Alportel. Check out the local ethnological museum on the left-hand side of the Tavira road.

On leaving São Brás, head north on the old Lisbon road that winds its way up through hillsides of cork oak, pine and eucalyptus. After 12km, at the intersection with the EN124, turn left towards Messines. After about 7kms, take a left turn as indicated to Querença, a hilltop oasis and a pleasant little place to pause a while.

From Querença, a riverside road signposted to Tôr emerges at a main road intersection. Turn right to Salir, which is back on the EN124. Heading west on the main road from hilltop Salir, an escarpment called Rocha da Pena comes into view on the right. Explore it on foot if you have time.

11kms after Salir, there is a turning into Alte with its *fontes* (springs) and Manueline church.

The EN124 carries on westward through São Bartolomeu de Messines, past row upon row of orange trees, until the castle looms into sight at Silves. Spend some time looking around the castle (9.0am-6.0pm), cathedral (9.0am-1.0pm, 3.0pm-5.0pm) and museum (10am-12.30pm, 2.30pm-6pm).

On leaving Silves, cross the bridge and turn right to get on to the A2 for all places east or west.

Other interesting drives are

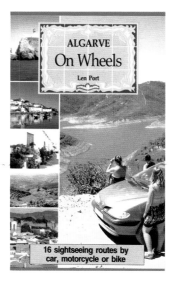

described in the book *Algarve on Wheels*, published by Vista Ibérica.

CYCLING

If you have gone to the trouble of bringing your own bike and you need spares or repairs, or if you want to hire a bike in the Algarve, ask at any tourist information office or check out the 'yellow pages' of the Algarve phone directory under *Bicicletas – Aluguer e Reparações.*

If hiring a mountain or trekking bike, check for saddle comfort; make sure the bike is well-maintained and that it comes with a pump. It should have a registration number and official document.

The tarred roads running east-west are fairly level. The EN125 is by far the busiest. The east-west roads inland have good surfaces and relatively little traffic. The steepest climbs are on the north-south roads running up into the serras.

The main things to look out for when road riding are manic drivers, badly surfaced roads and dangerously rough edges.

Headgear is important. Wear a safety helmet, or at least a hat as a shade against the sun.

There are plenty of refreshment points along the way, except in the sparsely inhabited northwest of the province and in the Serra do Espinhaço de Cão area where the roads are excellent for energetic cyclists.

WALKS

Local walkers have mapped out an 'Algarve Way' route from the Spanish border to the west coast. It is a serious trek, rarely undertaken at one go. Most visitors are content with single day rambles or easy walks lasting a couple of hours or so.

There is no network of designated footpaths and trails in southern Portugal as in many other countries, but this is not restrictive and much of the coastline and many areas inland are ideal for walking.

The only places closed to walkers are properties with *'privado'* signs and walls or fences obviously designed to keep people out. Elsewhere, provided you do not blatantly invade people's privacy, or cause damage to vegetation or crops, there is not a lot of concern about trespassing. There are hundreds of tracks leading along clifftops, across sand dunes, through farmlands, up river valleys, into woodlands and over hills.

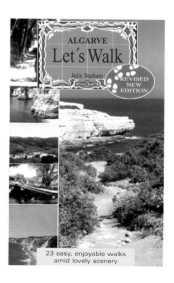

23 easy, enjoyable walks amid lovely scenery

The best clifftop walks on the south coast (east to west):

• Senhora da Rocha to Benagil via Albandeira and Marinha.

• Lagos to Salema via Ponta da Piedade, Porto do Mos, Luz, Burgau and Boca de Rio.

Some of the best countryside walks are in the vicinity of Alte, Paderne, Salir, Querença and São Brás de Alportel.

For hillsides walks, travel up to Monchique, Fóia, Alferce and Picota.

Algarve, Let's Walk by Dr. Julie Statham, describes 20 routes, none of them very strenuous. The author regularly leads small groups of visitors on outings (inquiries 282 698676 or 965753033).

Every walk should be a mystery tour. Unless you go on an organised outing, find a path in an area that takes your fancy and see where it leads to and what you come across along the way. Explore. Apart from sensible footwear, the only real concern is the weather. In summer, wear cotton clothes, not synthetics. If you anticipate being in the sun for any length of time, wear a hat and take along a bottle of water.

AIRPORT

Phone numbers:

Switchboard	289 808800
Flight information	289 800617
Lost property	289 800714
British Airways	289 800771
TAP-Air Portugal	289 808731

BANKS

Normal banking hours are Monday to Friday 8.30am to 3.00pm. Banks in all tourist areas prominently display the current exchange rates for major currencies outside the euro zone. The rate for travellers' cheques is slightly higher than for notes. Cash advances can usually be obtained with Mastercard, Eurocard, Access, Visa and other credit cards.

BUSES

Clean, reasonably comfortable and cheap. Local services are often infrequent by day and non-existent at night. Avoid long, boring journeys within the Algarve by booking express regional services. Good choice of Algarve-Lisbon bus companies and departure times.

CAR HIRE

Cars from reputable companies are clean, recent models. Drivers must be at least 21 and have had a licence for at least one year. Hire price always includes third party insurance. A government tax of 19% is a compulsory extra. Optional extras: collision damage waiver, theft insurance, personal insurance. Insurance does not automatically cover trips to Spain.

CONSULATES

Phone numbers:

British - Portimão	282 417800
Canada - Faro	289 880880
Dutch - Faro	289 820903
German - Faro	289 803757
Irish - Lisbon	213929440
S.African - Lisbon	21 3192200
U. States - Lisbon	21 7266600

DRIVING

- Have your licence and vehicle documents with you at all times while driving.
- Seat belts must be worn.
- Under 13-year-olds must not travel in the front seats.
- Car speed limits: in built up areas 50km/h; main roads 90km/h; motorways 120km/h.
- On arrival at a roundabout, give way to any vehicles already on the roundabout.
- Alcohol limit: 0.5gm/l, which is lower than in UK. Any fines must be paid on the spot
- If you are involved in an accident, exchange insurance details. If there is injury or serious damage ask someone to phone the police. The nationwide phone number for the police and ambulance is 112.
- Petrol stations are fairly plentiful along the south coastal strip, but scarcer on the west coast and the further inland you go. The only one on the A22 is near Lagos.

ELECTRICITY

220 volts AC with Continental two-pin plugs is usual.

EMERGENCIES

Police, fire, ambulance: dial 112 free from anywhere in the country.

LOST/STOLEN PROPERTY

To report or inquire about air travel baggage gone astray in transit, phone Faro airport lost property office 289 800714. Property lost in Portugal should be reported to the nearest GNR police station.

MEDICAL TREATMENT

Pharmacies (*farmácias*) will advise on minor matters. There are reciprocal arrangements within the EU on free treatment in clinics and hospitals. When requesting treatment show your passport, and an E111 or E112 form. Health clinics (*centros de saúde*) deal with less serious problems. For emergencies, there are 24-hour hospitals in Faro, Portimão and Lagos. Private doctors (English-speaking as well as Portuguese) will give more personal treatment, but without insurance it can be expensive.

POST OFFICES

Normal hours 8.30am-6pm, closed all weekend. Village post offices close for lunch. International telephone services available at all post offices.

SECURITY

Be every bit as security conscious in villas and apartments as you would be at home. When you go out, be sure to lock up. When driving, you need your licence and other documents, but don't leave them in the car when parked.

TELEPHONE SERVICES

Directory inquiries for Algarve numbers dial 118; for international operator, dial 171.

TOURIST INFORMATION

The Algarve Regional Tourist Board maintains offices in all the main tourist centres. They are a great source of all sorts of information, leaflets and maps. Use them, freely. Look for the black on yellow *Turismo* sign.

TRAINS

Express trains can be an alternative to buses on longish journeys like Vila Real de Santo António-Lagos or Algarve-Lisbon. Beware that some Algarve stations are quite a distance from the town or village whose name they bear.

WATER

Mains tap water is fine for cooking. Most visitors prefer to drink bottled mineral water.

As the Algarve is in a low rainfall area there is a general shortage of water, and so it is important not to waste tap water.

INDEX